the
Bridge
to Wholeness

the Bridge *to* Wholeness

A Feminine Alternative to the Hero Myth

Jean Benedict Raffa, Ed. D.

San Diego, California

LuraMedia™

LuraMedia
7060 Miramar Road, Suite 104
San Diego, CA 92121

Library of Congress Cataloging-in-Publication Data
Raffa, Jean Benedict.
    The bridge to wholeness : a feminine alternative to the hero myth
/ Jean Benedict Raffa.
        p.   cm.
    Includes bibliographical references.
    ISBN 0-931055-88-1.
    1. Individuation (Psychology)--Case studies. 2. Mythology--
Psychological aspects--Case studies. 3. Femininity (Psychology)--
Case studies. 4. Raffa, Jean Benedict--Psychology.   I. Title.
BF175.5.I53R
155.3'33--dc20   92-10643
                                                            CIP

Grateful acknowledgment is made to the following copyright holders
for permission to use their copyrighted material:

Cambridge University Press, for the quotation from *The New English Bible.*
    Copyright © the Delegates of the Oxford University Press and the Syndics
    of the Cambridge University Press, 1961, 1970. Reprinted by permission.
Harcourt Brace Jovanovich, for the excerpt from *Modern Man in Search of a Soul*
    by C.G. Jung. Reprinted by permission of Harcourt Brace Jovanovich, Inc.
HarperCollins Publishers, for the quotation from *The Kingdom Within: The Inner
    Meaning of Jesus' Sayings* by John A. Sanford. Copyright © 1970 by John A.
    Sanford. Reprinted by permission.
PARABOLA, The Magazine of Myth and Tradition, Vol. V, No. 4 (Fall, 1980), for the
    quotation from "Joseph Campbell on the Great Goddess" by Joseph Camp-
    bell. Copyright © 1980 by the Society for the Study of Myth and Tradition.
    Reprinted by permission from *PARABOLA.*

For my grandmothers, Fannie and Eliza;

For my mother, Verna, and her sister, Edna;

For my daughter, Julie;

And for Julie's friends: Susy, Emily, Kate, Lori, and Heather.

CONTENTS

ACKNOWLEDGMENTS

Several people read this manuscript in various stages of development. Some made helpful observations, some offered concrete suggestions, and some simply affirmed me as a person who had something important to say. I'd like to thank them: Rob Blakeslee, Carol Burton, Barbie Bynum, Debbie Gluckman, Beth Johnson, Dr. Marvin Kelly, Anne Meinecke, Dr. Jack Myers, Rick Raffa, Louise Franklin Sheehy, and Fr. Jim Shortess.

I'd also like to thank the members of my writers' group, Barbara Kennedy, Lenny Roland, and Peggy Smith, for their wonderful support and helpful advice. Thank you also to my very special fellow seekers, the members of my Centerpoint study group — Carolyn Coleman, Jean Hess, Emmy Lawton, Jane McCartha, Jane Nies, and Shirley Pipkin — for their acceptance and loving encouragement.

I owe a special thank you to Fr. Jim Shortess for helping me to see that my true talents do not lie in the masculine, scholarly realm of academia, but in the more subjective, feminine realm of women's issues and inner growth. I thank him also for his thoughtful reading of my manuscript and his affirmation of the soundness of its spiritual foundation.

I must also express my boundless appreciation to my Publisher, Lura Geiger; LuraMedia's Managing Editor, Marcia Broucek; and Copyeditor, Carol Sowell. Now I understand why writers need editors. The wise and insightful guidance of these gifted and caring women forced me to think and stretch and hone and shape until this book finally reached its present, deeply satisfying form. I don't like to think what it would have looked like without their help.

Finally, I have no doubt that this book would never have come into being were it not for the unqualified love and commitment of my husband, Fred, a rare man who has provided me with the space, both physical and psychological, to work and grow in my own way, in my own time. He has always been there for me, and I owe him more than I can ever say.

WOMAN

She starts life as a tender, budding flower
Pink and fresh with pristine innocence.
Eager to assert her female power,
She learns to value beauty over sense,
Thinking it her only real defense.

Anxious, she awaits the man she'll marry,
Knowing she'll feel safer by his side.
To her the world seems awfully big and scary
And she's afraid to walk alone without him as her guide.

Happily they join their lives together:
He to work and she to cheer him on!
Lovingly, she gathers silks and feathers —
Things to make their home a cozy nest
Where he'll want to come each night to rest.

Their first child is nature's greatest wonder
To a couple so uniquely blessed.
When the second comes she starts to ponder
Why someone who's so lucky should be tired and depressed.

Several busy years flow in succession.
He gains confidence and certainty;
She begins to think about oppression,
And to look for her identity,
Wondering when life will set her free.

So she starts a search for self-acceptance
In a world that values manly traits.
Painfully, she finds that independence
Will never come to one who only sits at home and waits.

If she perseveres she finds fulfillment:
In jewelled robes she leans upon a throne.
At last she's learned that freedom comes from being
True to gifts and talents of your own.
Now she's a creature who can stand alone.

But if she holds fast to the old lessons
Of inequality and prejudice,
Sadly, she joins the multitude of women
Who judge themselves, and all of life, with fatal bitterness.

J. B. R.

To every thing there is a season, and a time

to every purpose under the heaven:

A time to be born, and a time to die;

A time to plant, and a time to pluck up that which is planted;

A time to kill, and a time to heal;

A time to break down, and a time to build up;

A time to weep, and a time to laugh;

A time to mourn, and a time to dance;

A time to cast away stones, and a time to gather stones together;

A time to embrace, and a time to refrain from embracing;

A time to get, and a time to lose;

A time to keep, and a time to cast away;

A time to rend, and a time to sew;

A time to keep silence, and a time to speak;

A time to love, and a time to hate;

A time of war, and a time of peace.

(Ecclesiastes. 3:1-8)

A Feminine Alternative to the Hero Myth

THROUGHOUT HISTORY there have been many stories about the journeys of heroes. These fairy tales, myths, and other literary works have shown how male heroes strive to become their true selves. They do this by conquering cruel enemies, enduring difficult trials of strength, or slaying terrible dragons. The reward for all this hard work is relationship with the feminine: the hand of the princess or a return to the waiting wife. And this is where the story ends.

When a woman appears in a hero myth, her work is done for the sake of relationship. She may be a helper, a witch, a victim, a prophet, a seductress, or a reward for the hero, but she is almost never someone flowering as an individual.

According to most traditional mythology, a man's task is individuation, or becoming differentiated from everyone else by proving himself in personally fulfilling work in the physical world. If he succeeds, his reward is a return to the feminine. The combination of these two accomplishments (developing his individuality and achieving an intimate relationship with the feminine) allows him to become what he was intended to be and so to live out his destiny. In religious language, this goal is equated with entering the kingdom of God. In psychological language, it is called wholeness.

But for the female in traditional mythology, relationship is the only goal, and all her work must be directed toward maintaining relationships in the outer world. If this is not enough for her, it is too bad. As a result of this one-sided view, in the words of Joseph Campbell, ". . . there are no models in our mythology for an individual woman's quest. Nor is there any model for the male in marriage to an individuated female."[1]

For about five thousand years, Western civilization has emphasized what the Greeks called Logos, the active, "masculine" way of knowing and behaving. This is the way of the head — of conscious intellect, logical reason, active doing, and aggression. The qualities of Logos allow people to think clearly, develop their individual skills, and achieve success in the outer world.

When I say "masculine," I do not mean individual men or the male gender in general. Instead, I mean all the qualities that have traditionally been called masculine, regardless of whether they are exhibited by males or females. Unfortunately, men tend to identify solely with these "masculine" traits, and women with the opposite "feminine" ones. Therein lies the problem, and therein lies the theme of this book.

Western society has accepted the surface meaning of the masculine hero myth (by "myth" I mean a psychological/spiritual symbolic tradition) for so long that only recently have we begun to question the rest of the story. We are beginning to wonder what

---

[1] Joseph Campbell, "Joseph Campbell on the Great Goddess," *Parabola: The Magazine of Myth and Tradition.* Vol. V (4) (Fall 1980): 74-85.

happens *after* the hero marries the princess and develops a relationship with her. What is the next phase of his life like? What does it mean to return to the feminine? And we wonder what happens to the princess who is not fulfilled in living solely for her relationship with the hero. How does she acquire self-knowledge? How does she become an individual who develops her own potential? What is her story?

Until recently, few have noticed how utterly the masculine hero myth has neglected the feminine way of Eros, the way of *being* instead of *doing,* the caring, feeling, receptive, nurturing, life-affirming way of the heart that values relationships and a meaningful inner life. While our patriarchal society has given lip service to the feminine principle, in truth Eros has been considered inferior to the masculine way of Logos, and its true importance to the human soul has been largely disregarded.

Perhaps today the devaluing of the feminine can at last be corrected. It is up to contemporary women and men to tell new stories that will provide a more comprehensive picture of the meaning of life for future generations. These new stories must describe how one returns to the inner feminine instead of focusing solely on the outer masculine world of doing. They must show how women acquire self-knowledge by turning within to discover their own resources instead of depending on relationships with men for their salvation. And they must show how men perform the inner work that guides them to intimacy with the feminine — and thus to their own salvation — after they have acquired confidence and self-knowledge through the rewarding work of "dragon-slaying" in the outer world. These new stories will show that the way to wholeness for both men and women is a way that bridges the gap between masculine and feminine, Logos and Eros, individuation and relationship, light and dark, conscious and unconscious, the outer ego and the inner Beloved.

This book incorporates the neglected feminine element into our culture's collection of myths about the human search for wholeness: the quest for individuation integrated with the equally powerful need for relationship. At one level, this book is the story of one woman's quest for self-knowledge. In a broader sense, however, it describes a phase of the journey toward wholeness, i.e., a return to the feminine, whether it is experienced by the masculine hero or the feminine heroine. As I have described this experience, I have come to believe that, while men and women approach wholeness along very different roads, their journeys are alike in two important ways.

First, the journey always involves integrating the opposites within ourselves. When the inner summons to embark on a journey into wholeness occurs, the security that once came from conforming to the masculine, logical, outer world ends. Then the feminine phase of the journey begins. This is an inner, initiatory journey that involves the painful work of breaking through our resistances to growth and change — barriers that have functioned like protective walls — so that we can enter into the unknown territory of our fuller personalities and true potential. Learning to know and accept the opposites within ourselves, both the "bad" and the "good," brings about a powerful internal fusion in our personalities. This releases tremendous energy and makes us vitally aware of our connection to an inner, spiritual entity — God, the Self, the Beloved.

The symbol of the bridge helps us visualize this inward synthesis of the opposites. A bridge is an edifice that overcomes obstacles or gaps and connects things on opposite sides. In the human brain, there is a bridge called the corpus callosum that connects the verbal, highly conscious left hemisphere with the image-oriented, largely unconscious right. We are also familiar with the biblical rainbow, a bridge that overcomes the separation between humans and their creator, and unites them with a message of love from the spiritual world to the physical. I imagine another bridge, an invisible one in each individual that overcomes the artificial barriers humans have erected to separate Eros and Logos, the two fundamental requisites of every healthy personality. When we answer the call to both Eros/relationship and

Logos/individuation *and* can move freely back and forth across the bridge that connects the two, we are at last in a position to approach wholeness.

Most of us resist creating this bridge between the opposites in ourselves because we are afraid to face the painful inner realities we have spent our lives avoiding — truths like our terror of dying, our hidden hatred for ourselves and others, our fear of the unknown, our terrible selfishness, our desperate vulnerability, our closeness to the edge of the dark abyss, our agonizing need for love and understanding, our appetite for warring and killing, and our lust for power. What we do not realize is that these things must be faced before we can become complete, reborn individuals who know how to heal, build up, laugh, dance, love, and live in peace with ourselves and others.

The second common attribute of the journey of both men and women has been hinted at but neglected in the hero myth. We do, in fact, have a model for this phase of the journey, the uniquely feminine part of the story. The model is in the Christ story of sacrifice, suffering, death, and resurrection, but because of our contemporary focus on the outer world of rational, observable facts, we have lost touch with most of the rich inner meaning of this story. The journey that leads back to the feminine is an inner initiation into the unconscious, invisible, spiritual world. Whether it occurs in a man or a woman, it moves, like nature herself, through four phases.

The first phase begins when we are young and vulnerable, after we lose our initial innocence and total dependence on our mothers. The fear we experience at this profound loss makes us desperately needy for safety, so we spend our youth conforming: impressing our teachers, gaining the approval of our parents and peer groups, joining clubs, finding mates and jobs, and acquiring status, money, comfortable homes, and pat answers. Our need to conform is so powerful that we build strong protective walls, like the walls of a castle, around our true Selves, gladly sacrificing our real needs, even our own happiness, in order to maintain the illusion of safety that comes from yielding to conventional beliefs, roles, or authorities. Hiding in our sturdy, familiar castles makes us feel secure as we become independent from our mothers and adapt to the Father's world of work and group expectations. This time of seeking safety through conformity often lasts well into adulthood; for some it lasts a lifetime.

But some people gradually become aware of a strong inner torment, a feeling of being backed against a wall or of being torn between two seemingly irreconcilable allegiances, values, or duties. It is as if they hear a mysterious inner call to break free from conditions that formerly gave them comfort. Then the second stage of the journey begins. This is a painful time of leaving, a time when our need for safety is replaced by a stronger urge to retrieve the parts of ourselves that were lost during our time of conformity. During this stage we question old rules and break through our walls of resistance into new psychological and spiritual territory.

But just as hiding behind castle walls is not enough, neither is habitually leaving situations to chase through the wilderness every time we are unhappy. At some point we have to stop running, find a quiet place, and start the inner work of healing old wounds, facing our real Selves, and developing our true potential.

When we are ready to stop leaving, we move into the third stage, a time of profound metamorphosis, a time that some liken to death. Like wild animals that instinctively withdraw to die or give birth, we retreat to an isolated island deep within ourselves. There in dark seclusion we undergo the difficult work of exploring our unconscious realms. There at last we make peace with the opposite, hated aspects of our natures — all the terrible inner monsters we have spent our lives fighting and denying. There we learn that our personal dragons are not our enemies, and that confronting them will not be the death of us. It will only mean the death of our childish, immature selves who have to die so that a marvelous new Self may be born into our conscious lives.

The fourth and final stage is akin to leaving the island and crossing a bridge into the promised land of our full potential.

Bridging the barriers between the opposites frees us from so much that has crippled us and endows us with so much power and creativity that it feels as if we have been reborn into a fuller form of being. Then we reap the rewards of our arduous journey: increasing peace and serenity, growing intimacy in our relationships, and meaningful, creative work. We are resurrected — transformed from empty, lifeless, obedient puppets into fully alive, ever-expanding, unique individuals who are at one with ourselves.

These two characteristics of the mythic journey into wholeness — i.e., the integration of opposites and the fourfold nature of the journey — are the bones of this book. The following chapters add muscle and flesh by describing how I have experienced this journey. For many years I have kept silent about these things. Now it is time for me to speak.

This book is not just for women, many of whom will undoubtedly see themselves in these pages. It is also for men, who must learn how to return to the feminine, too, if they wish to approach wholeness. It is for everyone who is a seeker.

Epicycle: "The Lily and the Rose"

ONCE UPON A TIME there was a little princess who lived with her parents in a small castle near the edge of a vast forest. The forest was very dangerous, for it was full of wild animals. "If you will stay in the castle, out of the forest, and always be good, you will be safe," her parents warned her. So she was very dutiful and good, and in this way she managed to grow without harm until her eleventh year.

But one spring day in that year when the princess was bright with the confidence of youth and pink with the innocence of femininity, her mother, the queen, called her to her side.

"My dear child," she murmured with profound sadness. "Your father, the king, is dead. His kingdom was very small, and I am left with no money and no direction. I am tired and have few resources, but somehow we will survive."

The little princess said, "Don't worry, Mother. I am young and brave. I will never be a burden to you. I will go out into the world and find my own way."

Then the queen took something from the folds of her faded, wrinkled gown. It was an exquisite white lily, still moist from the morning dew. "Take this, my child," she whispered tenderly. "It is all I have to give you. If you keep the memory of this lily always with you, and if you search for it wherever you go, you will be safe."

So the princess wandered through the wilderness for ten years. Once in a while she would hear the roar of a dangerous animal, but she was always dutiful and good. And wherever she went, she searched for the white lily.

One evening just after dusk, she came to the shore of a river whose deep, churning waters glimmered like silver in the moonlight. In the middle of the river was an island on which stood a charming little hut. Over the door was a sign whose words she could just make out in the fading light. It said, "All Who Enter Are Free."

In the front yard was a large rosebush, and at the center of the bush was a single, beautiful red rose.

Something nameless stirred deep within the heart of the princess. A gentle warmth, like an ache, began to move through her body. Forgetting the lily, she moved slowly into the river. The raging current tore at her gown and wrapped it around her legs so that she stumbled and fell.

Just then, a huge honey-colored bear bounded to the edge of the water and stood staring at the princess, who was gasping for breath and struggling to regain her footing in the dangerous water. Behind the bear a man on a white horse came crashing through the undergrowth. It was the king of these lands, out on a moonlight hunt. Seeing the transfixed bear, he followed its gaze and spotted the princess. Immediately he leaped into the water, gathered the princess into his arms, and carried her to safety. And the bear disappeared into the woods.

When the bedraggled princess looked up at her rescuer, she saw that on his black jerkin was a crest, and in the center of the crest was a single white lily.

The king, who was called Peaceful Chieftain, carried the princess back to his castle, which was much like the one she grew up in with its high walls surrounded by masses of beautiful lilies. There they fell in love and were soon married. In time they were blessed with two beautiful children, a girl and a boy, and for a while their lives seemed complete.

But sometimes, to her secret shame, the princess still thought yearningly of the island with the little hut and the single red rose in the front yard. She tried to forget, but as the years went on she found that these thoughts occupied her mind more and more.

Occasionally the king caught glimpses of her sadness and, because he loved her very much, he looked for ways to erase it. One day he sent for a minstrel, who sang a song of freedom with such haunting beauty that the ache in the princess's heart grew to an unbearable intensity and she collapsed.

All the best doctors were summoned, but none knew how to cure the ache, and she did not have the words to tell them or her beloved husband the reason for her sickness.

One winter evening, the king was sitting by his wife's bed when they happened to glance out a tiny window that was set in the thick castle walls. There in the falling snow stood the tawny bear. Soon it lumbered off into the woods, and the agitated princess cried, "I must follow it. I must." And she dressed herself and prepared to leave.

"Then I will go with you," said the king. "I will protect you and keep you from harm."

But the princess was firm. "No, I must find the way by myself. But I promise that if you will trust me and wait, I will be back." The king's pain was very great for he could not understand her need, but because he hoped that this quest might cure her sickness, he sadly kissed her goodbye and watched her step out alone into the cold night.

The trail she followed wound on and on through the dark forest, and at times the princess feared that she would lose her way. But she knew that, until she found what she was looking for, she could not go back; for if she did, she would surely die.

At last she found herself once again on the shore of the river. There was the island with the hut and the rose. As the princess summoned all her courage for the dangerous crossing through the icy waters, the bear suddenly appeared beside her. Slowly it rose on its hind legs to its fullest height. Through the wintery darkness the eyes of the great beast glowed with a fierce yellow light, and its fangs and claws glistened in the pale moonlight. Fearfully the princess stood her ground and gazed into the bear's eyes.

It seemed as if the animal were speaking, and this is what she heard: "Have the courage to look deep and the boldness to act upon what you see."

Gently she reached up and grasped the fur on the neck of the great animal. Together they moved into the turbulent water and swam to the island.

When she reached the safety of dry land, the bear turned and, with a tender farewell glance, it swam back to the far shore and disappeared into the forest.

Trembling and alone, the princess walked into the hut.

For seven years the princess lived and worked alone in the hut. Gradually the ache in her heart receded and her health returned. Each evening after she finished her work, she would stand in front of the hut and gaze at the single rose on the bush. As she looked, she would remember the words of the bear: "Have the courage to look deep and the boldness to act upon what you see."

Then one warm spring evening as she looked at the rose, the words of her mother came back to her: "If you keep the memory of this lily with you, and if you search for it wherever you go, you will be safe." Suddenly a great wave of homesickness for the king, her children, and their comfortable, familiar home came upon her. She looked deep into her heart and knew what she must do.

Early the next morning, she rose from her bed and lovingly tidied the tiny hut. Then she walked into the morning sunlight, and there, by the light of day, she grasped the stem of the single red rose. As she picked it, she pricked her finger on a thorn and a drop of blood fell from her finger onto the stem. Where the drop of blood landed, a new rose immediately appeared.

Turning toward the river, she tucked the rose snugly into the bodice of her gown . . .

> Then, finally, she finds the perfect flower,
> And when she puts it on, at last she knows
> That other lives cannot impart their power
> To one who seeks the lily but whose essence is the rose.

Just as she was about to step into the water, an ancient arched stone bridge, polished smooth by the feet of many who had gone before her, appeared beneath her feet. With each step she took, it grew, and in this way, one step at a time, she crossed the river.

When she arrived at the castle, her family welcomed her with loving arms. The king held a great celebration, and everyone came from miles around to rejoice at the safe return of their queen. When the celebration was over, the queen used the rose to start a garden, and forever after the rose garden grew and thrived in the midst of the lilies.

Epilogue

EACH OF US HAS OUR OWN STORY. "The Lily and the Rose" is mine. Through the medium of the fairy tale, and with symbols and a plot that have meaning for me, I have tried to convey the essence of my particular journey. There is something about fairy tales that ideally suits them to this purpose.

A story says different things to different people at many levels of meaning. You need not understand the literal message of my story; I am not sure I understand it all myself. Just let the symbols speak to you in their own way.

I wish only to shed a little light on the title. For me, the lily and the rose symbolize the contrast between the two opposite natures that exist within each human being. The lily represents our active, aggressive, pure, objective, rational, idealistic, intellectual, masculine aspect — or Logos (what the Chinese call *yang*). All of us, male and female, have this aspect in our natures, but it comes more naturally to most males and tends to be more dominant in their personalities. In a patriarchy the masculine principle is considered superior to the feminine principle. Thus, the ideal masculine hero is the courageous, intelligent, spiritual, and spotlessly pure King Arthur or Sir Galahad; and the ideal woman, regardless of her true nature, is required to be submissive to the masculine principle and lily-white in her innocence and purity, like the Lily Maid of Astolat or the Virgin Mary — the patriarchal church's ideal of the perfect woman, whose symbol is the lily.

In contrast, the rose represents our passive, earthy, related, receptive, feeling, nourishing, compassionate, intuitive, instinctive, feminine essence — or Eros (*yin*). All of us have this aspect in our personalities as well, but patriarchies have long considered most aspects of the feminine to be inferior and undesirable. Thus, the feminine principle tends to be repressed in both men and women today. This is hard on everyone but especially devastating to women, because the feminine principle is the essence of our nature.

I accepted the authority of the lily at a young age, but it explained only part of my true nature. It has taken me half a lifetime to rediscover the equally potent authority of the rose. I know that only when the two are joined in an inner union can any person — female or male — hope to grow into wholeness.

PART ONE
A Time of Safety

1

Answers. Answers. Who's Got the Answers?

WHEN I WAS THREE YEARS OLD, my parents rented a vacation cabin on Lake Michigan. One evening as I played by the shore, I looked up to find that I was alone. Each parent, thinking I was with the other, had gone back to the cabin. I began to walk along the water's edge, following a distant pinpoint of light in the dark.

I still remember my feelings that, even now, are hard to put into words. Hurt: How could my mother lose me? Terror: Will she find me? Confusion: Is it possible that something bad could happen to me? Distress: Will somebody else find me and then will I have to live with them? Hunger: Who will give me food?

It seemed like forever, although it was probably only moments, before my father came up behind me, hugged me, and walked hand-in-hand with me back to our cabin. I was safe, but I was never again to experience the sense of utter faith and trust that I had lived with until then, for something new was set into motion that evening. I had become conscious of my existence in a very big, very dark, very dangerous world. Worse, I suspected my parents' fallibility. Was it possible they were not perfect and all-knowing? Why didn't my mother come for me? Didn't she know I would want her to find me? Why didn't my father carry me home instead of letting my brother ride on his shoulders while he simply held my hand? Did he love my brother more than me? Was it because my brother was a boy? Didn't my father understand how afraid I had been? Didn't he care about my feelings?

To the best of my memory, this event marked my separation from innocence and the beginning of my seeking and questioning. From this point on, I began to question the life I had been given. What were the rules? What must I do to stay safe? Who knew the answers?

For a while I continued to hope that my parents had the answers. Then, when I was eleven, my parents divorced. I sat in my mother's lap and cried and cried. How could this happen? How could it have been prevented? There were no answers.

Three months later my father died of his third heart attack. My devastating loss and the reality of death were too terrifying to face, and I still couldn't comprehend the idea of a dangerous world where my own existence might be in jeopardy. I desperately needed the illusion of a safe, benevolent universe, and I didn't have the courage to give in to my doubt and despair.

And so, in the way of wounded children everywhere, I denied these feelings. I didn't cry. I protected myself by building a wall around my emotions and believing that I was just fine. But the questions remained and there were new ones: How should I feel? How should I act? Should I look sad? How long was I supposed to mourn? Was it wrong to laugh if someone said something funny? Did everyone but me know how they were supposed to feel and behave when a parent died? Was there something wrong with me? Would this have happened to me if we were rich and famous?

My search went on. Perhaps someone other than my parents had the answers — maybe people like the President of the United States, or presidents of banks and leaders of business, or people who had achieved fame and wealth, like movie stars. But in my ninth-grade civics class I realized that neither the Founding Fathers nor current politicians had all the answers about how to run a country. They were just guessing, hoping, shooting in the dark. The same was true of business people. If wealthy financiers and knowledgeable economists could not keep the stock market from crashing, who could? And movie stars? Were they immune from pain? Gradually I realized that money and fame didn't seem to make any difference either. Famous people got sick, died, divorced, and had problems just like everyone else.

At seventeen, I turned to religion. I read the New Testament again and again. Ministers, saints, and youth group leaders became my authorities. And when the Reverend Billy Graham came to town and preached a powerful sermon and gave a compelling altar call, I was the first one to jump out of my seat and walk down the aisle. Now, I thought, I will find the answers through religion.

But as I learned the doctrines of my religion and followed the leaders I admired, I found that there were many religious leaders who believed in the same rules, yet came up with some very different answers. It seemed there were many ways of interpreting Holy Scriptures, many paths to paradise. And while I continued to live by the underlying truths I had found, there were no satisfactory answers to questions like: Why do good people suffer? Will faith in God protect me from pain? If it won't, what will? Why do I have to die? What is heaven like?

My search expanded into education. Teachers taught everything else; they must have the answers. But mostly I found theories, a major one being that I should learn to think for myself. How could that be? I was no expert. But I went as far as I could, and along the way I acquired more questions: Can people get better as they grow older or do they only become more corrupt? What should the purpose of education be? Whose fault is it when children fail in school? Their own? Their parents'? Education's? Society's? Is it possible for humans to create a perfect world? Who was right about what constitutes utopia? Was it Plato? Bacon? Rousseau? Marx?

And so I went from leader to leader, lecture to lecture, book to book, one castle of knowledge after another. Each time I searched for someone who had the answers, someone whose disciple I could be. And when each one disappointed me, I found a new authority to believe in, a new doctrine to conform to.

What was all this questioning really about? What was I really looking for when I sought answers from famous authorities and accepted doctrines?

All I wanted was this: a simple set of rules to live by that could protect me, like the thick walls of a cozy castle, from a terrifying, confusing world of loss, death, suffering, and loneliness. I wanted a predictable, uncomplicated world where I would be loved and understood and accepted and safe, a world where my mother would never lose me and my father would never die and I would never have to suffer all alone. A child's view of paradise — that is all I wanted. Nothing more. Nothing more.

2

Orphans

IN THE PHYSICAL SENSE OF THE WORD, I was not an orphan. Up to the age of eleven, I had two parents who loved me very much. After that, I only had one, but I still had warm memories of the other, and I still had family security. But in a psychological sense, there was a period in my life when I was very much an orphan. My time of orphanhood began with my momentary separation from my parents that night on the shores of Lake Michigan, and it lasted for many years.

It started with the realization that my mother was flawed, that it was possible for me to get lost, hurt, or worse, because the one person in the world who was the source of my security was not all-seeing and all-knowing. Suddenly I knew that I existed. I was separate from my mother. I was alone in the universe and at the mercy of dark forces. And I was terrified.

By the time my father's flashlight pierced the darkness, trust had been vanquished and a sacred wound had been born in my soul. Its name was fear. I say this wound was sacred because I believe fear is inevitable, and the suffering it causes is holy. Only when we have been wounded by fear and suffered its pain do we recognize that we are not sufficient, that we need help from a higher, divine authority.

Fear is what made me feel myself to be an orphan, and later, when my father died, fear reinforced my orphanhood and made it stronger and more pervasive. The worst fear of most orphans is abandonment, and that was my greatest fear at first. But when my father abandoned me by dying, I discovered that I could bear abandonment and, because of other things that happened at this time, I traded it in for a new fear: fear of exploitation. I, who had never met a stranger, who had always been confident, outgoing, and trusting, became very suspicious of others, especially men, because I believed they would hurt or betray me if given a chance.

Although I was certainly not consciously aware of my sense of being an orphan, unconsciously I was scared, hungry, and needy. I was scared to be bad, afraid of being punished by God. I was hungry for safety, for castle walls; for formulas that would ensure my protection; for the approval of my parents, my teachers, and God. I needed security, and when I was old enough to leave home and go off to college, I believed I would find that security in a man I could trust to love and protect me. I found the perfect man, and he carried me off to the safety of his castle, like a king on a white charger. I married him, and I demanded that he understand me, approve of me, and be a strong and dominant father figure, for only then could I feel safe.

For as long as I continued in this way, a period that lasted well into adulthood, I remained an orphan. Despite the love of a strong husband I trusted and the comfortable life we were able to provide for ourselves, despite my cheerful bravado in the face of difficulties and my insistence that I was tough and independent, despite our continuing good health and the birth of two healthy children, regardless of the security of my husband's job and the added security that a master's degree brought to me — underneath it all there lurked an orphan, an orphan who still didn't feel safe, even as queen of my own castle.

I still wanted authority figures to give me answers, to tell me what the truth was, and to save me from making mistakes. I continued to believe that if I was good, God would take care of me. I wanted permission from my husband and my religion before I dared to do something new or different. When they disapproved, I felt angry, but I rarely had the courage to rebel, for believing in these authorities was more important to me than my own desires. These authority figures made me feel safe and enabled me to deny my despair.

As an orphan, I had learned that I was separate from my mother, but even as an adult I still had no identity of my own. Because I did not know who I was, because I could not hear my own inner voice, I believed I must rely upon the good will of someone else to care for me. I did not believe in my own goodness, so I was willing to go to great lengths to trust, forgive, repay, and be loyal to my caregivers.

Luckily, the people to whom I gave my trust (first my parents, then my teachers and religious leaders, and later my husband) did not take advantage of my dependence, nor were they cruel or abusive. But if they had been, I still would have loved and defended them and their ways to the death. I would have had no other choice. An orphan must conform to the ways of those in authority, no matter how bizarre or unfair those ways may be; otherwise, there is no hope. To an orphan, conformity is the only way to stay safe, to survive.

Because I believed more in others than in myself, I denied my real needs. And as long as I sacrificed my real needs, I was doomed to be discontented, no matter how comfortable and secure the outward circumstances of my life might be. Had there been a lottery in Florida when I was in my orphan stage, I would probably have believed that winning it would solve all my problems. Certainly, like all orphans, I wanted a quick fix and an easy life and, although I could never have admitted it even to myself, I wanted it without having to work hard for it.

Carol Pearson, author of *The Hero Within*, says that in our journey toward wholeness, we all go through an orphan phase. Everyone has an orphan within. When we are young, and every time we are in unfamiliar situations or environments, it is our orphan who feels hurt, vulnerable, and dependent on others. No matter how loving or secure our home lives were in childhood, we all suffer a certain amount of disillusionment, anger, and fear when we begin to suspect that the world is not the safe place we had innocently believed it to be.

So we conform, because we believe conformity is our only hope of staying safe, the only way to avoid being abandoned outside of our castle walls. We cling to the customs and conventions of our caregivers with all our strength, never thinking to challenge the rules or stick up for ourselves. And we deny our despair and refuse to mourn; instead, like plucky little princesses, we put on happy, confident faces to convince ourselves and everyone around us that we are just fine.

Deep in our souls, we know we are not just fine. Yet we pretend because of a terrible secret we must hide from ourselves and others. The secret is that we are very bad, and our badness is the reason for our suffering. And why do we believe we are so bad? As orphans, we *have* to blame ourselves for our suffering; it *must* be our fault when bad things happen, because the alternative is unthinkable. Orphans are vulnerable victims who are not strong enough to accept the terrifying truth about the real grown-up world: that no one out there has the answers, that the forest is dangerous, that Mama is flawed and Daddy is dead, and that not even the thick walls of a castle can protect us from pain.

3

The Game of Hide and Seek

WHEN I WAS FOUR YEARS OLD, I did something I have never forgotten and am still ashamed of. I was feeling sick, perhaps I had a sore throat or an earache, so my mother took out a thermometer to take my temperature. I didn't remember ever seeing a thermometer before, so I asked my mother, a nurse, to show me how it worked. What were those little lines on the side of the glass stick? Would she show me how to read it?

Patiently she explained about the thin black line that moved up the glass cylinder from the little bulb on the end that was filled with something called mercury. This mysterious substance was not as hard as a ball or as runny as water, yet it acted like both. It could be broken apart into numerous little silver balls or united into one big, soft, silver ball, she told me. And she said you could rub some mercury on a dime and it would make the dime shiny, slippery, and silvery. The mercury was what expanded as it got warmer and made the little line that went up the thermometer. After telling me these things, my mother took my temperature, then showed me how to read the thermometer.

I was fascinated. Could I play with it for a while? I asked.

Well, I could hold it for a minute, but I must be very careful because it could break easily and then the mercury would spill out.

Oh, I would be careful, I promised.

Since I was normally a trustworthy child, not prone to making messes or having accidents, my mother decided to trust me, and she even left the room briefly while I pondered the mysteries of this fascinating new treasure.

The moment she left, I did not hesitate to act. Casually, I walked about the room. I allowed my mind to become a blank, to refuse to think about the deed that another, darker and unknown part of myself was contemplating. As I walked, I allowed my grip on the thermometer to loosen and the hand holding it to suddenly go limp as I "accidentally" tripped on the edge of the throw rug, a rug that had always been in the exact same place, a rug I had never tripped on before.

"Oh dear!" I said aloud, and my hands flew to cover my mouth in feigned surprise and dismay as the thermometer shattered on the floor beside the rug. When my mother came into the room, I was on my hands and knees searching for the little balls of mercury to roll together to make a bigger ball.

"It was an accident," I swore, believing my lie utterly and completely. "I tripped on the rug." Wasn't this the truth? Hadn't I indeed tripped on the rug? Hadn't my hands flown to my mouth in dismay as I uttered, "Oh dear!"?

My mother seemed disinclined to believe me and I was shocked. "It's the truth," I swore. "I tripped and it fell out of my hand and broke. I'm so sorry. I didn't do it on purpose. Honest!" And again I believed myself completely. I think I even managed to wring a tear or two out of my innocent, outraged eyes at the idea that my mother would think I would lie.

Being an instinctively wise woman with a deep-rooted belief that goodness would ultimately prevail in human nature if people were not forced into corners over small and insignificant matters, my mother let the subject drop. Together we picked up the shattered pieces of the thermometer, threw them into the trash basket, then rolled the droplets of mercury into a single ball and rubbed it on a dime to see how it would shine.

Deep within me, a tiny, ugly creature crouched in the dark corner to which it had been banished by the conscious, "good" little girl I believed myself to be. I could not acknowledge the presence of this "bad" girl for I was afraid of being punished. So I began to build a wall in front of it so neither I nor anyone else would see it. Soon it no longer existed for me.

When I was in the first grade, something else happened to remind me of this unwelcome creature. One day the teacher announced that in a few days we were all to have blood tests. I don't remember the purpose of the test. I just remember Miss Berry telling us that we would go to the school nurse who would prick our fingers, squeeze out a drop of blood, apply it to a glass slide, and then we would go back to our rooms. It wouldn't really hurt very much, she said. Just a momentary pinprick. We must take these permission slips home, have them signed by our parents, then bring them back.

That afternoon as I rode home on the school bus, I made my mind into a blank. I would not let any words or ideas form in my head. Almost of its own volition, my right hand crept into the pocket of my dress, where it found a small crumpled piece of paper. I didn't let myself think what it was. It was simply a scrap of paper. I looked in determined fascination at the passing scenery, ignoring the hand that secretly tore the permission paper to shreds in the darkness of my pocket. I shifted the pieces of unimportant paper into my left hand, which moved slowly and casually to the open window. I looked at the chattering, fidgeting children in the bus and forced myself to smile and speak to the person sitting next to me (usually I never bothered to speak to anyone on the bus, preferring to keep to myself) as I ignored the fingers that casually opened and allowed the scraps of paper to slip stealthily between them into oblivion.

Miss Berry was surprised when I said my mother had decided not to sign the paper. Since Mama was a nurse, I said, she'd take care of pricking my finger herself. As I sat alone in my corner of the classroom watching my classmates file back from the school nurse, each with a cotton ball between thumb and middle finger, the tiny creature in the dark corner inside myself was a little bigger, a little uglier. But I ignored it and the deep sense of shame it caused me. I chose instead to continue to think of myself as a good little girl. I built my wall a little higher to cover this growing creature, and I breathed a sigh of relief because I had escaped the pain of the finger prick.

Such is the morality of youth. Issues like truth, honesty, and other people's property are not very important to vulnerable little girls for whom the most pressing need is to survive with a maximum of need fulfillment and a minimum of personal discomfort. At this, the earliest level of human morality, "good" to a child is anything that keeps her out of trouble, gains the approval of her family, and gets her what she wants. "Bad" is anything that causes her pain, gets her into trouble, or prevents her from fulfilling her needs.

Thus, although even at the age of four I knew that I shouldn't break the thermometer and that I should tell the truth about what I had done, my need to satisfy my curiosity, quickly followed by my need for self-preservation, was simply more powerful. At six, although I knew it was wrong to lie to my teacher and not to tell my mother about the blood test, my need to avoid pain had top priority. Because these needs were so strong, I had no recourse but to ignore and deny the truth that I knew at a deeper level: I had broken some rules that were important to the adults in my life. I had lied. I had been bad.

And so, like all children, I learned to play the game of hide and seek. Hiding my secret badness behind a wall of denial became a way of life for many years. I came to believe that because I conformed in public, and because I sought and gained the approval of the people in power, then I really must be good, regardless of how I thought or acted in private. In other words, I didn't know how to separate the game I played and the mask I presented to the world from the way I really thought and acted when unobserved by others, which, of course, was not always "good."

There is nothing abnormal about concealing the truth about ourselves and acting from motives of self-preservation when we are very young. In fact, research into moral development indicates that we all pass through this stage as we wander through the murky forest of ignorance toward the light of moral maturity. Only we must be careful not to stay there overlong. If we do, what was normal in a young child becomes very dangerous as we move into adulthood, for then our inability to see the truth about ourselves or reason from any standard other than self-protection can cause much greater damage to ourselves and others.

It was my powerful need for safety that caused me to seek the protection of castle walls when I was a child. Every time I lied to avoid punishment or hid the truth about myself to gain the approval of others, I added another brick to the wall that kept the real me safely hidden away where the world could not see and judge and condemn. But all my attempts to hide could not prevent my other half — the rosy-red child who was a real person and not a paragon of purity — from blossoming in the secret darkness of my soul, while on the outside, my lily-white child basked in the light of the approval I so desperately sought.

4

The Betrayal of the Feminine, or
The Year the Lone Ranger Shot Me

WHEN I WAS TEN YEARS OLD, I had a dream I will never forget. It was one of those "big" dreams that has a powerful emotional impact on the dreamer and can be a prefiguration of the essential problems and direction of one's life.

> *I'm walking along the railroad tracks near the home we lived in when I was five. The tracks wind through the dark woods. I am alone. Suddenly I hear somebody come up behind me and call my name. I turn and see that it is Tonto.*
> *"The Lone Ranger wants to see you," he says. "Come with me."*
> *I'm thrilled. The Lone Ranger is my hero. When I grow*

up I want to be like him. Tonto is his faithful Indian guide and friend. The Lone Ranger trusts him with his life, and so do I.

I follow Tonto back along the tracks to where the Lone Ranger stands waiting. His magnificent horse, Silver, is grazing silently behind him. The Lone Ranger speaks to me. "Stand down there by the tracks," he says. So I walk down the embankment beside the railroad track and stand there with my back to it, waiting in excited anticipation to see what wonderful thing he will say or do.

Silently he pulls his gun from his holster, points it at me, and pulls the trigger. In shocked amazement I gape at him, uncomprehending. Then I grasp my stomach where I've been shot and think to myself, "Now I will die." In terror I begin to scream, waiting for the life to seep out of me. Surely I will fall over and die any second. But I don't. The Lone Ranger stands there, cool and detached, watching as I scream and wait for the death that never comes.

I woke up screaming with my heart pounding wildly. When I finally understood that it was a dream, I began to cry. My mother came to comfort me, but nothing helped. Even awake, I felt that I had been mortally wounded.

As indeed I had been. At the age of ten, I had suffered a betrayal by the most beloved symbol of goodness and justice that existed in the society into which I had been born. It was a betrayal I did not understand at a conscious level but which nevertheless was to shape the next thirty years of my life. The wound I received was a mortal blow to a fundamental part of my personality: the innocent, delicate, confident, hopeful, feminine little girl child who had truly believed she was just as acceptable and equal as everyone else, who thought she had just as much chance to grow up to be like her hero as anyone else.

The Lone Ranger was a hero, all right. As a character in comic books and on television, he defended the poor, the weak, the powerless, the innocent. He rescued victims. He stood for everything that was right and good and brave. But the Lone Ranger would not be a role model for me, and I could never be like him. Girls were victims, not heroes. He had delivered the killing, silver-bullet blow that spoke for the entire patriarchal adult world he represented.

"This is what you get for daring to think you can be like me," this blow said. "I am a hero for boys who will grow up to be men and run the world. It's time you understood the difference. You aren't important, you're only a girl. The only way you will ever be accepted is to play by men's rules in a men's world. Maybe if you work hard, we'll let you win once in a while. Maybe if you're good, we'll take care of you. Maybe if you're lucky, you'll get to bask in the reflected glory of a powerful man. But that's the most you can ever hope for, so don't be a fool and think you're special. You'll never be special in your own right. You're only a girl."

Here's how I know now what that gunshot at the age of ten meant:

That was the year I began to develop breasts.

That was the year I realized that when my brother flexed his muscles my parents were impressed, but when I did the same they were embarrassed.

That was the year I stopped wrestling and racing with the neighborhood boys . . . and winning.

That was the year a minister immersed me in a baptismal tank and assured me when I emerged that my soul was saved from uncleanliness and eternal damnation because I had submitted myself to the authority of the patriarchal church and the masculine trinity of God the Father, God the Son, and God the Holy Ghost.

That was the year I tore up the thirty-page novel I was writing because, when I realized how difficult a task it would be, I lost confidence in the ability of a mere girl to succeed at it.

That was the year that, in order to please my father, I agreed to be reasonable on my birthday and trade my passionate wish for a horse for the more practical and affordable riding lessons he promised me instead. I never got either one.

That was the year I gave up my plan of being a veterinarian and decided instead to be a nurse.

That was the year I learned about sex and decided I would be a good girl and a virgin so I would be respected and treated well by God and all the important, powerful people: the men.

That was the year I stopped trusting men.

That was the year I sold my soul for their approval.

That was the year I learned that if I conformed to the masculine image of femininity, that if I sought only the lily and shunned the rose, I could preserve my safety.

That was the year I betrayed my own divinely ordained destiny — my femininity. It would be approximately thirty years before I would begin to recover this, the greatest loss of all.

5

Eros Repression: Sexual Obsession

EROS, THE FEMININE PRINCIPLE of relationship, is the life-preserving instinct, and sex is one of its major manifestations. It is Eros that gives us the energy to keep up the struggle for survival. The energy inherent in Eros is so potent that it can empower the human spirit to build glittering, diamond-studded bridges to the moon, to the stars, to the divine, to eternity. If thwarted, if prevented from finding a healthy outlet, Eros energy simmers in unconscious cauldrons. There in dark secrecy it concocts monstrous Mr. Hydes and Jack-the-Rippers who lurk behind walls and crouch in dark alleys, waiting for vulnerable victims upon whom to unleash their misdirected energy in the only way left open to them: destruction and death.

Eros acknowledged, Eros revered, Eros celebrated in joyous

gratitude is chocolate, champagne, a Chopin nocturne, perfume. A soft warm bed — shared. A newborn kitten. Life.

Eros repressed, Eros denied, Eros mishandled is self-hatred, rage, rape, anorexia. Suicide. A silver bullet, a bomb, a dagger, a derringer. Death.

For a very long time, Eros has been repressed and Jack-the-Ripper has been winning. So it was when I grew up in the 1950s. In those days when the puritanical double standard reigned supreme, the sexual aspect of Eros was rigidly controlled. In the hands of male authorities, sex was a socially sanctioned weapon that men used to maintain their control and repress the feminine. The rules were strict and clear: Unmarried teen-age males had license to experiment or not as they chose (although few freely admitted to the latter). For females there were only two choices: "Bad" girls did and "good" girls didn't, and that was all there was to it.

By the time I became a teen-ager, there was no doubt about which kind of girl I would be. My protected environment; the spoken and unspoken rules of my society; the tender care I had received from loving parents whom I deeply respected and had a strong desire to please; the quaint, old-fashioned books my mother gave me, in which none of the heroines was ever kissed until she became engaged; my own introverted nature; and my fear of a punitive masculine God — all these things made it easy for me to be an extremely innocent, eminently "good" girl. I believed it was important to conform to the unspoken rules, to keep my mind pure, my feelings and emotions repressed, and my hands clean.

So I pushed my natural Eros (an anagram for rose) nature way down deep within me and surrounded myself with a carefully constructed wall built of all the things I thought would keep me safe: obedience, innocence, spirituality, passivity, purity. And even when I ventured out of the castle to wander in the dangerous wilderness of adolescence, I always carried the image of the lily with me, for the lily was my talisman, my ideal, and I believed that as long as I sought it, I would remain safe.

For the most part I did remain safe, but not completely, for there was one important reality that in my sheltered innocence I had failed to consider. It was the reality of prejudice, of humankind's abiding fear of and hostility toward the opposite and the unknown. Because I lived in an era when the masculine way was considered to be superior, the feminine was regarded as inferior. Thus, men *had to* severely repress their own feminine aspects, and women *had to* be kept under masculine control at all costs. Women who wished to be acceptable to the mainstream of society were limited to three roles: lily-white virgin, supportive wife, or devoted mother. Any other way of being feminine was forbidden.

This prejudice against the feminine meant that all women, even those who accepted these roles, were susceptible to being victimized by insecure men who feared the feminine. But the most susceptible were women who threatened, thwarted, or resisted the masculine (either the masculine principle or an insecure individual man) in any way. In those days it was still true that women (like people of color or other minorities) who challenged the status quo or dared to step too far out of the prescribed roles would be self-righteously punished by the outraged advocates of the prevailing patriarchy. These advocates could be either males or females, and the punishment could range anywhere from hostility, verbal abuse, or ostracism all the way to physical threats, violence, or even murder.

I had two experiences with this kind of prejudice during my teen-age years. Both involved the issue of sexuality, a particularly potent realm for an impressionable, developing teen-age girl, especially one who wanted so badly to be safe and acceptable. Both very effectively did exactly what they were meant to do: keep me submissive to the masculine principle.

The first occurred when I was twelve, several months after my father had died. One day I was home alone after school when the phone rang. When I answered it, a man's voice asked for my mother. When I said she wasn't there, he said, "You'll do." Then he proceeded to tell me, in vulgar, sexually explicit terms, exactly what he wanted to do to me. Having been trained to always be polite to adults, I listened. When he was finished, he said, "I'll be right over."

"Okay," I said, in a tiny, respectful voice, and as I hung up the phone, my hand trembled so violently I could scarcely replace it in the cradle. With my heart pounding in my throat, I raced out of the house and across the street to Inez's house.

Inez was my surrogate mother and the mother of Jimmy, my childhood sweetheart. I spent hours at her house every day, talking, watching the "Mickey Mouse Club" and "American Bandstand" on TV, helping Jimmy with his homework, ironing his clothes, and watching Inez cook and clean. It was from Inez that I learned what a housewife was. We were so close that I never even knocked on her door. And she was always there.

She was there this day when I flung myself breathlessly into her house and told her about the phone call. She went into action immediately. First she called my mother at work. Then she called the police. Then she called the next single woman listed in the telephone book after my mother's name to warn her that she might get an obscene call. I spent the rest of the afternoon at Inez's house, peering anxiously out the window from time to time and expecting to see a strange car pull up to my house.

For months after that day, I couldn't answer the phone if I was home alone. And if the doorbell rang, my mother or my brother would have to see who it was. I was simply too afraid it might be my obscene caller and that if I went to the door alone he would snatch me up and carry me away before my mother could save me.

This was my first glimpse into the dark and evil recesses of the human soul, and the impression it made on me was profound and lasting. My father's death had already made me fearful. After that phone call, the masculine gender became the focus for my fear, and I became shy, suspicious, and withdrawn around boys and men.

My second experience of masculine prejudice against women

involved another telephone call. One evening in the summer before I was to enter high school, a girlfriend was at my house when the phone rang. It was a boy who wanted to talk and flirt but who wouldn't tell me his name. The memory of the obscene call three years earlier was still very much with me and, holding my hand over the phone, I told my girlfriend I didn't want to talk to him. My friend, however, was a bold and sassy girl who had no fear of boys and was delighted by my phantom caller. Taking the phone away from me and speaking in a shy and quiet voice, she continued to talk to him as if she were me.

At first this game was fun, and she would put her hand over the phone and whisper what he was saying and we would giggle and then she'd talk some more. But soon her side of the conversation began to make me uneasy. Her voice was sounding more seductive and her laughter more sensual. When I asked her to tell me what he was saying, she wouldn't say. I began to get frantic. I didn't trust my friend or this strange caller, and I begged her to hang up and I tried to grab the phone away. But she resisted me and kept her hand over the phone so he couldn't hear my voice in the background as she answered his questions with coy and sexy monosyllabic affirmations that kept her voice disguised. When she finally hung up, I asked her what he had said but she refused to tell me. After a while I gave up asking and decided to forget the whole uncomfortable incident.

That fall we entered the tenth grade, and soon I went to my first high school dance. It was marvelous. The shy little wallflower I had turned into during junior high school seemed to be blossoming again at last, for I was dancing with a boy, and he seemed to like me. And he was cute! During an intermission he took me by the hand and led me across the dance floor to a wall of boys standing on the other side.

Among them was a boy I'll call Ken. Ken and I had gone to the same elementary school. One year we had been in the same class and, according to a friend, he had developed a crush on me. Every Wednesday we had folk dancing in our physical education class. Ken had asked me several times to be his partner, but I had refused because I always danced with Jimmy. I had no sense of how my rejection of Ken might have hurt him. I only knew I didn't feel comfortable dancing with anyone but Jimmy.

The years had passed and we had gone to the same junior high school. We no longer had any classes together, but every once in a while Ken would call me. By then I had become very shy with boys, even boys I was interested in. And I was still not particularly interested in Ken. He must have sensed this for eventually the calls stopped.

At the high school dance, my new friend said hello to Ken, then moved on to talk to someone else. Face to face with Ken, I smiled and said hello.

Ken looked at me with a cold and venomous stare before he very quietly and deliberately spat out a single accusing word.

"Pig!"

The smile froze on my face as I looked at him in shocked bewilderment. I had no idea why he'd said that, but the pain of his obvious and intense hatred was excruciating. As soon as I could, I excused myself and ran to the girls' room. I locked myself in a stall and remained there sobbing for the rest of the night, refusing to come out until the party was over and everyone had gone. Then I crept quietly out into the dark night and climbed into my mother's waiting car in the beautiful new white dress I had worn so proudly to the dance. I was never able to wear that dress again without feeling dirty and ashamed.

There is more to this story. Gradually this event receded from my mind as I moved through high school. I regained some of my earlier confidence and trust, and in the summer after my junior year, I spent two weeks with my cousin in Georgia, had my first summer romance with a wonderful young man, and received my first kiss. In the fall I dated a few nice boys and even let two of them kiss me good night after several dates. But there were no sparks between us, and it wasn't until the end of my senior year that I finally had a real boyfriend, a boy I'll call Steve. My relationship with Steve lasted throughout the summer and into the fall, when I went off to college and he went to the local junior college. We continued to write, and both of us looked forward to seeing each other again over the Christmas vacation.

One night during the holidays, Steve told me he had been invited to the house of a man to whom he was distantly related by marriage. This man, who had specifically asked Steve to bring me along, had occasionally felt the need to offer a little fatherly advice ever since Steve's stepfather had died a few years ago. Coincidentally, although Steve and Ken had never been friends, this man happened to be Ken's father.

I went reluctantly, fearing to see Ken, who had not spoken to me again after the tenth-grade dance. I was relieved to find he wasn't at home. Steve and I talked with Ken's father for a few minutes, then he asked to speak to Steve alone. When they came out, we left.

I asked Steve what Ken's father had said. At first Steve was reluctant to say, but finally he told me that Ken's father had said, "You don't want to get serious about a girl like that, do you?" With a sinking feeling I asked Steve what he had meant by "a girl like that," but deep in my heart I knew. Somehow Ken still thought of me as a tramp — a girl who had kissed exactly four boys in her life (unless you counted the time Jimmy had snatched a kiss from me during a neighborhood game when we were in the second grade) — and he had conveyed this belief to his father.

Ken's father's intervention worked. It sowed suspicion in both our hearts, and Steve and I broke up during the Christmas holidays. A few weeks later when I met a very attractive man, I was free to encourage him. He was my future husband. Isn't it odd the way fate works?

I pushed these painful memories deep into the recesses of my brain for many years. Then one night about ten years ago, I had a revelation so potent that I sat straight up in bed in amazement. Suddenly everything was clear. *Ken* had been the mysterious caller that my girlfriend had flirted with as she pretended to be me! He had whispered obscenities to her, playfully at first, and instead of being shocked and afraid as I would have been, my feisty friend had amused herself by encouraging him.

Ken was a well-intentioned young man of the 1950s who was brought up to believe in the sexual double standard. It was okay for boys to enjoy vulgar sexual repartee, but good girls just didn't do it. He had liked me as long as I fit the acceptable stereotype of an unobtainable, lily-white virgin goddess. But when this image was shattered by "my" behavior on the telephone, he became convinced I was a slut!

Both Ken and my earlier obscene caller believed the masculine principle was superior to the feminine — in other words, they were prejudiced. The underlying cause of prejudice is fear. What we fear, we hate and try to control, and we build strong walls to separate it from ourselves, in both our inner and outer worlds. When the walls get too thick and high — in other words, when the side that seeks control is not mediated by knowledge, understanding, and acceptance of what it has banished to the other side — the dominant side becomes obsessive in its mistrust of the other side, and in its fascination with it.

Thus, when the masculine principle, which is normally aggressive anyway, is not mediated by the softening effects of the feminine principle, which it rejects, two things occur. First, violence against the hated "other" (any aspects of femininity that are not sanctioned by the patriarchy) becomes rampant and tolerated. This is why so much sexual abuse of all types is perpetrated against women, even innocent, well-meaning women who conform to, perhaps even defend, patriarchal rules.

The second result is a growing obsession with the thing we fear and wish to control — in this case, female sexuality. This is one of the reasons for the constant emphasis on "sex" in advertising, the media, popular music, and other aspects of our culture. And it helps explain why those who vehemently preach against pornography and prostitution often end up patronizing both.

No matter how well I conformed to the only acceptable role

that was available to me as a teen-age girl, that of lily-white virgin, and no matter how much I repressed my fuller feminine nature by building a strong wall around it and seeking only the lily (patriarchy's interpretation of what a woman should be) — it was not enough to erase prejudice against the feminine. My castle walls could not protect me from an abusive telephone call from a sexually obsessed male, and my search for the lily in the adolescent wilderness could not keep me safe from the scornful, self-righteous judgments of a teen-age boy and his father.

But I was too young and insecure to question this injustice. I still needed to believe that castle walls and lilies could shield me from harm. So throughout my teen-age years and well beyond, I continued to conform to Logos-legislated laws and to judge myself by Logos-inspired standards. In the process I deprived myself of my birthright: my rosy-red Eros nature.

6

High School Popularity

WHEN I WAS A TEEN-AGER, I liked to read the teen magazines and advice columns. A big issue then was popularity, and all the articles said the same thing: The way to be popular is to "Be yourself." That always frustrated me. What kind of advice was that? What did it mean? I was looking for guidelines and helpful hints on what to do, and all I got was "Be yourself." I had no idea how to be myself. I didn't even know what it meant.

So I studied the kids who were really popular to learn what made them that way. Many of them came from wealthy families. It seemed that getting a new Corvette for your sixteenth birthday was one way of being popular. But since I came from a family that was barely making it, that way was closed to me.

Another thing I noticed was the way they looked. Most of

the extremely popular kids were very attractive. Their hair was thick and beautiful, their clothes were stylish, and their bodies were perfect. But basing popularity on the way people looked seemed so unfair to me. Nobody could help the way they were born. Besides, there were a few kids who weren't beautiful at all but were still popular. I rejected the emphasis on appearances as being unjust and too incomplete an explanation. There must be something else.

Then I noticed that many of the "in" kids had total confidence in themselves. They seemed to say and do exactly what they wanted to, often hurting others in the process. It was so easy for them to look down on others and call people hurtful names. Nevertheless, they were admired because they had a certain self-assurance and strength of personality that attracted others like a magnet.

In my inexperience I equated their callousness with their popularity and found that one was too high a price to pay for the other. I couldn't bring myself to approve of their snobbery or to cultivate a superior attitude just to be popular, so I began to experiment with the idea of not even trying.

It took me a long time to understand that I was doing what the advice columnists meant when they said "Be yourself." Now I know they meant to listen to your inner voice and be true to it. But at seventeen, it's hard to trust your inner voice when it deviates from the accepted teen-age standards. I thought there must be something wrong with me for not conforming to the norms and for having, heaven forbid, that worst of all possible failings: being different.

What I didn't realize as a teen-ager was that these gifted, confident kids did have part of the answer. They already had a pretty good idea of who they were and what they could do, they were comfortable with their youthful values, their confidence in themselves was attractive to others, and it was easy for them to be themselves. It was just that in their immaturity they hadn't yet learned tolerance or compassion. Because life had given them so many natural advantages, they had no idea what it was like to feel insecure or different, so they tended to be thoughtless and judgmental. In their heady enjoyment of their gifts, which they assumed made them naturally superior to those who lacked them, and in their desire to conform and be popular, they were oblivious to the pain they caused others who didn't fit the teen-age pattern for popularity, a pattern that valued conformity to outward expectations, and appearances over being true to the realities of the inner Self. The roots of this tradition go back a long way.

In ancient Greece, the temple at Delphi was dedicated to the god Apollo. On the wall of this temple, Apollo's special motto — an ancient prerequisite to the modern "Be yourself" — was inscribed. It said, "Know thyself."

One might wonder why, since the beliefs of the ancient Greeks have had such a profound influence on the Western world, humanity has yet to figure out how to attain Apollo's goal of self-knowledge on a broad scale. Perhaps it is because Apollo was second to Zeus, his father, and Zeus was guided by the precepts of power and authority and the hierarchical notion that there was room at the top for only one. For Zeus, power was far more important than self-knowledge and, unlike self-knowledge, which Apollo believed was available to all, power was a scarce commodity that only a few could possess.

Things have changed a bit since ancient times. Now many people worship one god instead of several, but to most of us God is still very much a masculine father figure. We say we value self-knowledge and authentic behavior, but these things are still secondary to Zeus's model of power and authority, a model that popular culture teaches us to look up to as the highest and best to which humans can aspire. As a result, our heroes are those who are powerful, who look good, who win, who are confident and skillful enough to get to the top, who prove that they are "better" than everyone else, who appear to have everything under control, who never seem to be plagued by guilt or self-doubt, who conform to the accepted notions of success, who hide behind tough walls that cover up troublesome feminine natures that crave caring and connection.

Conformity is a castle that conceals authenticity and stifles individuality. A castle is a strong and impressive fortress; if it were not, most of us would not grow up dreaming of living in one. But the illusion of safety and the pleasures of power and prestige a castle provides cannot compensate for the withering of the soul of the individual who insists on remaining within its walls. Moreover, the castle cannot prevent crisis; it cannot teach us to recognize the call of the Golden Bear; it cannot prepare us for the island ordeal. As long as we remain within its walls, we have no hope of completion.

But castles have a seductive charm, especially for the young, the weak, the innocent, the needy, the fearful. So most of us conform: We keep climbing and comparing ourselves to those around us to see who is higher, looking up to those above us and looking down on those below. These are the rules by which we play, and each time we play we devalue ourselves and each other because by insisting that someone has to be on top, we reinforce the belief that the rest of us are losers.

My high school was a castle fit for a powerful Greek god; Zeus would have approved heartily. No one seemed the least bit concerned with self-knowledge. School rewarded and punished us in direct proportion to how high our grades were on paper-and-pencil tests. It gave us no help in plumbing our psychological, spiritual, or ethical depths, and paid little attention to the development of individual gifts other than academic or athletic ones. In this system the ability to lead a meaningful life and achieve peace with ourselves and intimacy with others went unnoticed and unrewarded. In fact, school was a place where "Being yourself" was far more apt to get us punishment than praise, both from the authorities and from our peers.

Even organized religion turned out to be a castle constructed on Zeus's creed. As far as I could see, most religions empowered men and restrained women, valued lofty spirituality at the expense of earthly physicality, and judged and condemned all who fell short of the "one true faith." Moreover, every church had its own special list of taboos — for some it was dancing, for others it was drinking wine or playing cards on Sunday — and individual church members who saw nothing wrong with these things and dared to be different had to hide the truth from the critical, judging eyes of their neighbors.

In fact, as a teen-ager it seemed to me that practically the whole adult world continued to embrace a high school mentality. Most of the adults I knew were far more concerned about constructing, displaying, and hiding behind splendid castle walls than they were about being real. I knew no one who had broken through the walls, no one who was on a search for self-knowledge, no one who dared to be too different!

And so, like almost everyone else I knew, I continued to conform to Zeus's model of power and outward appearances during my teen-age years. At least on the surface. After all, this was the way the whole world seemed to be organized. Who was I to question it?

But at the same time, I was becoming aware of some conflicting ideas and feelings deep inside me. How did the admonition to be yourself fit in with this model? Why did the teen-age pattern of popularity seem so unfair to me? Although I still didn't know who "myself" was, I knew without a doubt that there were some parts of my innermost Self that were different from the norm. I was too fearful and needy to expose these things to the world. Yet some of these aspects of myself were becoming more and more important to me.

I had always believed that conforming was the way to stay safe — and staying safe was still my deepest need. But adolescence and high school presented me with conflicts that made staying safe far more complicated than ever before. I was discovering that neither living in a castle nor following the lily could quiet my disturbing questions or protect me from discomfort. And I was beginning to realize that, somehow, the castle of conformity was no longer quite as satisfying as it once had been.

7

The Role of Wife: Hera

SEVERAL YEARS AGO my husband and I were invited to a party at the home of some people we had recently met. Halfway through the evening I was sitting on the stairs, sipping my drink and people-watching, when a man I didn't know came and sat beside me.

As we made small talk about the hosts and the music, I began to realize that he was flirting with me. I'm not really great at flirting, so I was a little uncomfortable. But I didn't want to be mean, so I kept my manner friendly and matter-of-fact.

After a time, three very intense women walked solemnly to the foot of the stairs, sat in a semicircle on the floor, and stared coldly and silently up at me. The hostility that emanated from them was almost visible. I tried to include them in the conversation, but they simply sat and glared.

I felt awful. I realized they must be friends of this man's wife — perhaps one of them *was* his wife — who were banding together to intimidate this new female whom they saw as a threat to his wife's security. I had done nothing provocative, yet these women were obviously furious at me for being the object of this man's attention.

That seemed so strange to me. They were not mad at the man, who obviously had an unsavory track record. They were mad at me, another woman, though I had done nothing but be friendly and polite. Apparently it didn't matter that they themselves had probably been in similar situations in which strange men had made unwanted advances. I don't think it occurred to them that his flirtatiousness might make me feel uncomfortable, just as it might make them feel. They seemed to feel no kinship with me whatsoever. Our femaleness was not a basis for understanding and compassion — it was grounds for suspicion and hatred.

In Greek mythology Hera, the long-suffering, loyal wife of the powerful, philandering Zeus, was the same kind of woman as the women at the foot of the stairs. When Zeus deceived and seduced the innocent maiden Callisto, Hera in her jealous rage turned Callisto into a bear, which she then plotted to have Callisto's son kill. Zeus got off scot-free. This sort of thing happens again and again in the Greek myths.

Of the seven major Greek goddesses, Hera is the one I have always liked least. Oh, she had some wonderful qualities: She was constant in her respect for the marriage bed, and her fidelity and commitment were admirable. But she was so darned spiteful and miserable, and her relationship with her husband was so filled with hostility and tension! Her single-minded devotion to her role of wife and her power struggle with her more dominant partner in that one-sided relationship prevented her from establishing any real intimacy with him and blinded her to the innocence of any woman who might unwittingly capture his interest.

I've always disliked utter dependency and vengeful spite in human wives, too. Why don't they get a life of their own? I'd wonder. Where is their self-esteem, their independence, their pride? This was what I thought about the three women at the party. I was hurt by their irrational behavior and angry that they blamed me without knowing anything about me.

What I didn't realize until recently was that Hera's jealousy and vindictiveness are symptoms of a deeper reality about a specific feminine archetype: Hera represents the kind of woman whose entire existence is defined by the role of wife. A woman like Hera lives for her partner, and she will automatically subordinate everything, including her pride, her needs, her own opinions, and her relationships with others, in the interest of maintaining her wifehood. Unless she has a good dose of the qualities of a few other goddesses as well — goddesses like Athena, the active intellectual, or Demeter, the nurturing mother — a wife can end up like Hera, sacrificing everything in order to preserve the increased status and power she acquired by accepting the role of wife, and forever punishing her partner and other women in her frustration and rage at the limitations of this role.

My growing awareness of Hera's willingness to sacrifice everything to hold onto her partner came about because of a dream I recently had.

I'm outside looking at my house (totally unlike my real one). Someone has set off a bomb in the foyer, and it has blown the roof off. It starts to rain and the house is flooding. I'm afraid everything will be ruined, so I decide to save as much as I can. The first place I go to is our bedroom. When I open the door, I see a lavish, comfortable, beautifully furnished room with thick carpeting; exquisite paintings on the wall; a huge, shiny-clean, tiled bathroom; lots of closet space; and lovely, warm, peaceful colors. I realize in amazement that this room that I share with my husband is in perfect shape, so I go to check on the rest of the house.

On the other side of the house near the front door are three bedrooms for guests. They are white, sterile, and sparsely furnished. As I go through the house, I realize that the only damage is to the roof over the foyer. Nothing else is hurt in any way.

This dream took place shortly after an experience in which I had "blown my top" at another person, someone with whom my husband was actually more annoyed than I was. Normally I'll do almost anything to avoid a confrontation, but in my loyalty to my husband I said some things that hurt this person. As a result, the roof over the foyer, the threshold to the outside world and the people in it, was damaged and in need of repair. And the guest bedrooms, the rooms where I might house and entertain friends and relatives, were somewhat cold and sterile. But the bedroom I shared with my husband was exquisite and in perfect shape.

As I came to understand this dream, at last I realized the truth about myself: Although I have always thought of myself as being independent and self-sufficient, I am actually very much like Hera! It doesn't come out in the same way, since I'm usually not jealous or possessive, but I have just as much of Hera in me as those three women at the party had in them, for I too have always tended to put my husband first. *(Chink! go the bricks as they are added to the wall of the castle.)* In fact, for the first several years of my married life, I put my husband's needs ahead of my own to such an extent that any time our needs conflicted, I always sacrificed my own in favor of his. *(Chink! "It's not nice to be selfish; you should always put other people first.")* On a conscious level, I thought I did this because I loved my husband. Moreover, I believed that self-sacrifice *(Chink!)* and martyrdom *(Chink!)* were praiseworthy, and that this was the way good wives were supposed to be *(Chink!).*

But our conscious, professed reasons for doing anything are rarely the whole story. The Father religion and my patriarchal society had done their job. Without realizing it, I was putting my husband first because I believed he was more important than I was.

All my life, society had taught me that men were the doctors;

women, the nurses. *(Chink! "Hide that intelligence; cover up that ambition; it might offend a man.")* Men were the bosses; women the secretaries. *(Chink! "Let the men call the shots; men don't like bossy women.")* Men gave the orders; women followed them. *(Chink! "Do what you're told without complaining or people will think you're a bitchy troublemaker.")* Men were heroes and authorities; women were victims and servants. *(Chink! "Cover up your strength; don't be a know-it-all; men like women to be soft and submissive.")*

I put my husband first because I needed the security and status that living in a king's castle brings to women in a male-dominated society. I had little hope of acquiring such a powerful fortress on my own. I put him first because I needed the safety of thick castle walls to protect me from dangerous bears and turbulent streams and haunting visions of island huts. And I put him first because I had no idea who I was, no idea that I was someone other than a wife, no idea that the reason for my existence and the meaning of my life did not hinge solely on my relationship with my husband.

Because of my lack of self-knowledge and my powerful need for safety, submission and sacrifice became a way of life for me after I married. Every time I sacrificed something that was important to me, I added another brick to the wall I continued to build around my real Self.

Naturally, this resulted in some problems. Since it seemed to me that my husband always got his way and I rarely did, I began to feel like a second-class citizen in our relationship. It was inevitable that in my mind he would eventually become "the bad guy," which of course he did, just as Zeus did in Hera's mind. After several years of marriage, I grew to be pretty angry. During all this time it never occurred to me that he only got his way because I gave it to him on a silver platter and almost never insisted on my own!

Consciously, I believed that my sacrifices and self-denial were the purest form of love, but unconsciously, my true motivation was safety. I thought I was nurturing my husband and protecting him from my selfishness, but in truth I needed my castle walls more than I wanted to be true to myself. Self-deception is a dangerous shield; the only thing it nurtures is anger, and the only thing it conceals is truth. For as long as I denied my true needs, my anger grew. I was in the grip of a classic case of "Hera possession," a state where I was willing to neglect my own needs and sabotage other relationships because of the one relationship that was of utmost importance to me. And I didn't have a clue!

8

Horse-Crazy

WHEN I WAS A CHILD, horses were my passion. I saw my first horse one warm summer evening when I was five years old and my father took me for a walk down a dusty Tallahassee road to a nearby stable. I fell immediately and passionately in love. From that day on, I went to the stable as often as I could. It was bliss just to be near these magnificent animals — to see them, smell them, touch them.

My goal in life was someday to have a horse of my own, and every year as my birthday drew near, I grew more and more excited as I fantasized about the horse I would find outside my window on the morning of my birthday. I continued to have this fantasy even when we moved to a house within the city limits of Tampa.

Throughout elementary school everyone knew I was horse-crazy. In the fifth grade our class published a newspaper, and my contribution was a running serial about a black stallion and his herd of mares. When I was elected president of this same class, I organized a drawing contest. Naturally, I entered a picture I had drawn of a beautiful stallion. Naturally, I won the blue ribbon. By the age of eleven, I had read all the horse books in my school library. My favorites were the Black Stallion books by Walter Farley.

One day in the summer before the sixth grade, I wrote myself a letter to open when I was sixteen. With the letter I included the best present I could think of to give my future sixteen-year-old self: a picture I had drawn titled "A Wild Stallion Sniffing the Air." It showed a stallion standing high on a cliff overlooking his herd of mares far below.

That winter my father died, and my hopes of getting a real horse of my own were crushed. There was no way my mother could afford such an impractical luxury, and I had to be content with a rare trip to the local stable where, if I was lucky, the owner might take pity on me and give me a free, informal lesson.

By my twelfth summer, my youthful passion was beginning to fade. My father's death had sobered me up a great deal *(Chink! go the bricks as they are added to the wall: "Daddy can't protect you any more; you'd better play it safe!")*, and I had begun to lose my unrealistic dreams *(Chink! "Playtime's over; it's time to grow up!")* and my utter confidence in myself *(Chink! "Face it, kid; you're a victim!")*. Nevertheless, when I spent a month of that summer with some of my mother's relatives in Michigan, I was elated when my uncle leased a black-and-white pinto to be mine for the duration of my visit, and I loved every minute I spent with my precious Boo.

During my high school and college years, my love for horses took second place to my newfound interest in boys. Then at twenty-one I got married and began to dream about having a child of my own. But the horses were still there, running around in the shadowy summer pastures of my mind, and I still dreamed of owning one someday.

After five years of marriage, my husband bought me a horse to compensate for the lack of children in our lives. Bamboo was a beautiful, creamy white, blue-eyed gelding — a dream come true for me. But the dream was short-lived because a few months after we bought him, I became pregnant and was warned by my cautious doctor not to ride during my pregnancy. We sold Bamboo a few months before the birth of my daughter.

Thus ended my passionate love affair with horses. Thus began my role as mother. It was the only thing to do, for motherhood is a full-time job.

Isn't it?

When we grow up, we learn to be reasonable and give up our unrealistic childhood dreams.

Don't we?

Passion is a foolish and dangerous emotion.

Isn't it?

It can be very enlightening to look closely at the symbols that prevail in our conscious, outer lives. They often have an amazing correspondence to the status of our inner psychological development. In my outer life, my youthful confidence and self-sufficiency were symbolized by my fixation on the black stallion, the epitome of powerful masculine energy, combined with dark, feminine, instinctive passion. As a girl I contained within myself the potential to develop all the capabilities of this powerful symbol; but, unfortunately, its wildness and darkness were not quite acceptable to a world that prefers reason to passion and masculine to feminine.

Thus, as I grew older and began to submit to the demands of the world I lived in, my symbol acquired some balance and became a tamer, more reasonable, and less passionate (lighter-colored) black-and-white pinto. *(Chink!)* Finally I grew up to accept the restrictions that a patriarchal society places on women. I traded the castle of my parents for the castle of my husband, and my symbol became a lily-white gelding with blue eyes. Passion and dark femininity were lost, and masculine light and reason were paired with the instinctual energy of the horse. *(Chink! Chink!)* But I lost even that when I sold my horse, quit my job, and prepared to accept my role as mother. *(Chink!)*

I gave up any ideas I might have had about following my passion. As I had grown into adulthood, instead of tearing down the walls and growing into a fuller, more authentic person, I had simply added more bricks. By then I had developed the skill of a mason as I applied brick after brick to the wall surrounding my real Self.

At the time I sold my horse, it seemed that I had only given up my obsessive love for horses, but in my psychological life this renunciation symbolized much, much more. What I surrendered as I grew up was my authentic, passionate, unique feminine Self — a Self that was intelligent, confident, literary, spiritual, independent, and idealistic about using my skills for the betterment of others in some meaningful way. I traded this Self in for the security to be found in the occupation of elementary school teacher *(Chink!)* combined with the traditional role of wife *(Chink!)* and, later on, mother *(Chink!)*.

In choosing to be a teacher, I was guided principally by my strong need for security and societal acceptance, not by my real interests or skills. And although becoming a wife and a mother were the right choices for me, I was not completely happy in either capacity because I entered a struggle to conform to an ill-fitting, societally transmitted rendition of these roles instead of being true to my Self. I put my relationships first, and I continued to look outside my Self for answers and confirmation. It never occurred to me to tear down my protective wall and look within to see what was really there. And every time I pleased others instead of being true to my Self, every time I sacrificed something that was important to me for the sake of a relationship with someone else, the thick wall surrounding the real me grew higher and higher.

Recently I had a dream.

I am in a kitchen with a friend (a woman who personifies motherhood to me). We are standing before a low, double-

*doored freezer in the middle of the room. As we open and close
the doors, getting things out for a dinner party, my friend
accidentally bumps the head of a young, dark-haired boy who
is standing close between us. The boy, who seems to be
between the ages of ten and twelve, starts to cry. I think she
should kiss his head where she bumped him. But then I realize
she has children of her own and knows how to handle this, so
I say to the boy, "She has children of her own." The dark-
haired boy looks up at me and stares deeply into my eyes and
says, "Yes, but does she have a stallion?"*

In real life, the woman in my dream is someone who has
devoted her life to being a wife and mother in the manner in which
our society has traditionally defined these roles. Because she was
in my dream she represents a part of me, a part that once believed
(and perhaps still does): "Motherhood is a full-time job. Isn't it?"
(Chink! More bricks in the castle wall.)

Like the woman in my dream, I grew up believing that
relationships with my husband and children would fulfill me and
thought I must give up my other dreams in return. "When we
grow up, we learn to be reasonable and give up our unrealistic
childhood dreams. Don't we?" *(Chink!)*

When I submitted to the dictates of my society about what
kind of job was appropriate for me and how to be a wife and
mother, I gave up my horse — my passion. "Passion is a foolish
and dangerous emotion. Isn't it?" *(Chink! Chink! Chink!)*

This does not mean there is something wrong with being an
elementary school teacher or a wife or a mother. It is just that for
me, these roles were too confining. Some women do not find these
roles confining. Not every little girl is horse-crazy like I was. Some
little girls are doll-crazy or boy-crazy; some are born to be mothers
or teachers of small children; others find their deepest happiness
in being wives or lovers. For other women, their truest essence is
best expressed in work that does not gravitate around relationships with husbands and children. Some women are born to be

spiritual guides or scientists or artists or athletes or attorneys or professors or mechanics or writers.

One might assume that because passion is such a powerful emotion it must be associated with the light of reason and the active masculine principle. But this is not so, for passion comes from the Latin word *passio,* which means suffering, or being acted upon. Thus it is associated with the passive principle, the one that is being acted upon — e.g., the Passion of Jesus Christ — and not the active principle that does the action. When one has a passion, one is acted upon by a calling from or to some unknown greater power — a calling that cannot be ignored without endangering one's very soul. Moreover, passion is synonymous with emotion, and emotion is associated with the dark, feminine, dangerous side of our natures, as distinguished from reason and light.

Passion, this very feminine quality, is indigenous to human nature and essential for life satisfaction. Dangerous it may sometimes be and often in need of taming but, like the feminine, it is also life-giving and life-affirming and must be honored in each individual if we are to find the meaning of our lives. Each of us, male and female, needs to learn to find and trust and follow our passion. We need to acquire the necessary self-knowledge of what our passion is, and then we need to develop the courage and discipline to pursue it. The only way we will ever feel good about ourselves is by living our lives fully instead of hiding from our true potential. This is the meaning behind Horace's saying, "*Carpe diem,*" or seize the day. It is also what Joseph Campbell meant when he told his students to follow their bliss.

When I told the little boy in my dream that my friend had children, he said, "Yes, but does she have a stallion?" It is possible that for my friend, her passion for her children is enough. Perhaps she will never hear the compelling call of a Golden Bear. But the little boy who looked me straight in the eyes is my own inner little boy, and he knew that once I was horse-crazy. He knew that I was the kind of woman who needed more than relationships with a husband and children: I needed my stallion, too.

9

Encounter with the Wall

IN MY EARLY THIRTIES I began to suspect I wasn't happy with my life. I had no idea what was wrong with me. I only knew I was dissatisfied and I could think of no earthly reason why. I had everything I had been taught to want. I'd spent my entire life being a good girl, being in total control of every aspect of my outer life, making my family and mentors proud of me, becoming a good wife and mother, doing everything that was expected of me — and doing it well!

But I didn't like myself. I didn't know myself. I didn't know how to be myself. I didn't know what I wanted or what would make me happy. I had no idea that there was much, much more to me than the sweet and smiling feminine face I had appliquéd, stitch by painful stitch, onto the real fabric of my being.

My awareness of my unhappiness made me feel guilty and ungrateful, so I tried hard to ignore these unacceptable thoughts. Usually I succeeded, but occasionally my dissatisfaction would break into my consciousness in a powerful way, and I'd be forced to see my pain. Then I had to acknowledge that something was preventing me from being the person I wanted to be.

I didn't understand it yet, but I was feeling a powerful call to throw off the stereotypes, defy the old prejudices, and find my true Self at last, whatever that might be. But that seemed so dangerous, and my prison wall was so familiar, that I felt a tremendous resistance to breaking out of it. The tension caused by a powerful desire for change on the one hand, and a terrible fear of changing on the other, was unbearable. At times I thought I must be going crazy, as if I were launched on a path to destruction, as if something evil within me was compelling me to wreck everything I'd worked so hard to build.

What I didn't know was that I was experiencing a normal phase of adult life. But I was right in sensing danger, for this is a time when the potential for wreaking havoc is at its peak. Many people, especially women, lapse into depression when they come up against their walls. Some divorce their spouses or quit their jobs. Others lose themselves obsessively in projects or work. Still others abuse drugs or quietly drink themselves into oblivion every night. Members of either sex look for a return of happiness in the arms of a new lover, or simply get into bed with as many as they can.

It takes time to see the walls we have erected and gain the confidence to break through them. In the meantime the suffering can be so intense that all a person can think of to stop the pain is to escape. Leaving, in fact, is necessary, but it is crucial to understand that what is called for is an inner leaving, not an outer one. What we must leave is our childish state of dependency — all the old habits, fears, and resistances that have kept us from growing into wholeness — and not necessarily a physical situation in the outer world. Sometimes an outer leaving is also necessary. But mental escape — through drugs, alcohol, blame, or denial — is never the answer. Perseverance is of utmost importance if one is to overcome the seemingly insurmountable problems at this time of life.

Some of us fail to see our walls because we are unwilling to suffer. Or we are too afraid of losing the approval of family and friends if we expose our real Selves. We may simply be too emotionally fragile to endure the trauma of honest, shocking self-revelation. I think all of this and more was true of me during this phase of my life. I had painstakingly built my wall over many years by sacrificing my real Self, and it was very hard to give up the illusion of safety and "having my act together" that this habitual approach to life gave me. It was hard to see that I had outgrown my wall and that, instead of protecting me, it was beginning to choke the life out of me.

Like a shell that covers a tender growing embryo, my wall had served two functions. Its hardness had protected me from the condemnation I was sure I would get from the outer world if people knew what was really inside. And its thickness had kept the light of consciousness from entering in so that, in my fragile vulnerability, I would not have to see myself as I really was. I was truly in the dark, not only about my faults but also about my potential. But I was ready to grow up at last, and the wall-induced darkness that had felt protective for so long began to feel like a trap.

The hidden world on the other side of my wall contained at least two major parts: the realm of my true feminine essence (which, although frightening, was comprised of an unimagined abundance far exceeding the limited stereotypes of the outer world) and my largely untapped masculine aspect. It was my growing awareness of the presence of these two unknown facets of my personality, coupled with my resistance to exploring them, that caused my discomfort.

Finally, in an attempt to do something about my unhappiness, I decided to go back to school for my doctorate. Unknowingly, this was a decision to develop the second realm behind my wall: my untapped masculine, or Logos, aspect. This was when my quest for individuation began in earnest. In the tough, masculine world of academia I would be forced at last to think for myself, rely on my own skills, confront my faults, and seek my own truths instead of always depending on others for help and answers.

By developing my inner masculine aspect — all those qualities I had relied on the men in my life to have — I would acquire Logos/light (consciousness) to enable me to see the wall, Logos/energy (the ability to act for myself) to help me break through it, and Logos/courage to face the monsters on the other side. In a one-sided world where women are discouraged from being heroes, I had failed to develop these qualities on my own. I desperately needed them to rescue my feminine essence, that other part of my unconscious that slumbered behind thick castle walls. She would be my glorious reward for the difficult trials I would have to endure.

I had no clear idea that I was embarking on such a quest. But slowly, slowly, as I went through the doctoral program, I began to see that, although I might be very different from my husband, different from other women, *I still had value.* It was okay to be me, maybe even desirable! I began to see that I had been hiding my true Self and my real potential behind the wall.

PART TWO
A Time for Leaving

10

Into the Woods

SOME SEASONS AGO there was a delightful musical on Broadway called "Into the Woods." It was based on three favorite fairy tales — "Little Red Riding Hood," "Cinderella," and "Jack and the Beanstalk" — and a fourth one about a baker and his wife. In the first act everything happened as it should and everyone lived happily ever after — but only for the duration of the intermission. During the second act, things began to go wrong and the audience found out what happens *after* "happily ever after."

For example, the giant's wife came to the village to seek retribution for the death of her husband. Jack and the villagers ran into the woods to hide, but several innocent people were killed — all because of Jack's heroic deed. And Prince Charming, feeling trapped in marital bliss, started leaving Cinderella and their baby alone at the castle while he went into the woods looking for adventure. What he found was the baker's wife, with whom he had an affair. Similarly, Charming's brother, who had rescued and married Rapunzel, also went into the woods where he rescued (and romanced) first Sleeping Beauty and then Snow White.

All those who had done what they thought they were supposed to do in the first part of their lives — and who therefore assumed they would be safe and happy forever — suddenly found themselves having to deal with dark and unexpected urges, needs, and consequences. They had to go "into the woods."

Even though this Broadway comedy pictures the "call to the woods" in the extreme, for many of us there does come a time when we are called by a strange new force, like a mysterious Golden Bear, to leave the safe and familiar and enter the woods. This usually occurs during midlife, and it signals the end of the time when we need to submit to authority and adapt ourselves to society's expectations. Although it is painful and frightening, this call to the woods is a sign that we have acquired enough confidence and strength to separate ourselves from the old, outmoded ways and begin our initiation into a new, more mature, more authentic phase of life. If we have the strength to answer the call, we will eventually emerge as happier, more fulfilled people. If we refuse the call, we will simply be called again and again, as we go further along the road. The longer we delay our journey into the woods, the more urgent the call becomes and the more destructive the consequences are apt to be.

The call of the Golden Bear can be experienced in many ways. It usually begins while we are still safe in the castle. It may start with a vague yearning for something indescribable that seems to be missing from our lives. Gradually this becomes a growing awareness that we are unhappy with ourselves, our jobs, or our relationships. Or we may be confronted with a problem that we can no longer solve in the same old ways. Or the call may be a temptation to do something we never dared do before, a need that can no longer be ignored.

Sometimes we experience an exterior crisis over which we have no control — like the sudden appearance of an alien giant who, by invading our lives and killing our spouse or putting our company out of business, leaves us without a mate or a job. Although the exterior crisis may be nothing more than a cruel, senseless accident and not an inner call from a benevolent force beyond ourselves, its overall effect can nevertheless be beneficial if it forces us to grow — to question many of the assumptions about life that we have taken for granted, and to change our behaviors in positive ways or take on new roles we might never have considered before. The adjustment can be very difficult, but if we are able to persevere in facing and understanding what is before us, the ultimate results of this kind of devastating experience can be positive and life-enhancing.

At other times the call comes less dramatically from within. Our tiny inklings of unhappiness and dissatisfaction simply grow and grow until they reach such gigantic proportions that we begin to see the person, role, job, belief system, or institution we thought would save us or give our lives meaning as a villain or tyrant. Thus, Cinderella feels bored and unfulfilled, and thinks it is the fault of the prince and their child. Prince Charming feels trapped by his marriage. Red Riding Hood thinks her parents are uptight and repressive. The baker hates his job and the unjust economic system that forces him to stay in it. The baker's wife is mad at the church and the priest because they did not help her enough in her time of need. In other words, we convince ourselves that what we once thought was so good is now so bad that we need to leave it. This can take the form of an outward separation or an inner, mental change of attitude.

Reaching this discomfort or dissatisfaction is a crisis point, a time when we must choose either to continue to respond to an uncomfortable situation or condition in the same way we always have, or to take charge of our lives and do something different and unexpected — something that feels like stepping out alone into the woods and exploring who we are on our own terms. If we do not leave our "villains" behind, we will continue our resentful, dependent status and never achieve an authentic relationship with our villains or our true Self. Usually we can make this separation, or change of relationship, mentally, but for some a physical break is necessary.

Although our journey into the woods almost always at first appears to be a cruel accident or a dangerous and foolish mistake, it can be the bravest and best thing most of us ever do. In fact, making the journey to follow the Golden Bear through the wilderness to find our authentic Self is the only real hope we have of living "happily ever after."

11

Forks in the Road

"WHEN I WAS A CHILD, my speech, my outlook, and my thoughts were all childish. When I grew up, I had finished with childish things" (I Cor. 13:11, N.E.B.). This quote from the Bible suggests that becoming an adult involves more than simply growing bigger and older. It means choosing to stop behaving like a child and to start behaving like an adult. There is nothing easy about doing this. In fact, it is probably the most difficult thing we ever do.

For Beth, growing up meant that after two failed marriages she decided to stop believing she had to have a man in her life to be happy and to start finding out who she was without one. The idea that she might spend the rest of her life alone terrified her, and sometimes she was so filled with anxiety that she could barely function. And yet a deeper, wiser part of her knew that this change was something she had to endure, that she was in the process of tearing up a road map she had followed all her life and creating a brand new uncharted course for herself.

For Brad, becoming an adult meant breaking the pattern, handed down to him by his father, of expecting his wife to meet his every need, while treating her needs as unimportant. This new attitude subjected him to ridicule from some of his buddies, but he began to realize that he cared more about her feelings than their approval.

For thirty-year-old Stephi, it meant deciding to stop blaming her critical, perfectionist mother for her weight problem and accepting responsibility for her own destructive eating habits. Instead of focusing on wounding her mother, she began to focus on healing herself.

For Alan, it meant choosing not to blow up in a jealous rage every time his wife of nineteen years noticed another man, and to begin trusting and being supportive as she struggled in confusion through a painful midlife crisis.

For Erica, it meant refusing to believe her father and her boyfriend when they said she was stupid and deserved the abuse they gave her. It meant facing the fact that the ones she loved were cruel and unloving. She began going to a therapist to learn how to stop being a victim.

For James, becoming an adult meant facing his dislike of his job and realizing that he would rather do something else, even if it meant alienating his family or accepting a less luxurious life-style.

For me, it meant deciding to act on all the restlessness I'd felt for years instead of dismissing my pain and passively waiting in my safe, cozy castle for something to happen. It meant taking my powerful inner proddings — the call of the Golden Bear — seriously, even when I didn't understand where they came from or what listening to them would mean for my life. It meant deciding to stop constructing a wall, brick by brick, around my true Self in an effort to stay safe by conforming to rules and roles and standards that were not right for me. It meant tearing down some of those bricks and making choices to be true to myself, even when I thought I might be wrong and even though I risked encountering the displeasure of those I loved, instead of living my life for the sole purpose of pleasing others.

It meant breaking away from my narrow, self-imposed prison and going back to school to earn my doctorate, an act that felt like entering an unknown wilderness filled with dangerous choices. Each new choice I encountered was like a fork in the road where I had to stop and decide whether to continue to follow the Golden Bear deeper into unknown territory or to return to the safety of the castle.

For example, when the time came to write that first term paper, it was extremely difficult to overcome my lethargy, my natural inclination to procrastinate or spend a minimal amount of time and energy on this disagreeable task. In my reluctance to follow the Golden Bear — in other words, to commit myself to overcoming my passivity and doing the thinking and research necessary to develop my writing skills and write a really good paper — I found myself wondering why I should work so hard at something that was so difficult. Wouldn't it be easier to run back to the castle where my work was familiar and easy and non-threatening?

Other forks in the road involved my reluctance to risk discovering some very frightening things about myself: for example, that I might not have what it took to persevere at difficult work for a distant goal, or that I might not be as intelligent or capable as I had always believed I was, or that I was so flawed that not even getting my doctorate could make me happy. Why not take the road that would lead back to the castle, where I could rebuild my wall so I wouldn't have to face those terrible possibilities?

As hard as some of these choices were, the most difficult of all were those that concerned my relationships with those I loved. Was I really justified in risking damage to those relationships by insisting on pursuing paths that forced us to reorganize family roles, priorities, and expectations? Was I merely being selfish? Was it unnaturally cruel, perhaps unfeminine of me, to continue to follow the Golden Bear and make my family confront situations and decisions that were often difficult for them? Wouldn't it be better, perhaps more admirable, to fall back into the old familiar role of childlike, princess/mother/wife who ignored her own pain and took care of everyone else so they wouldn't have to suffer?

Each of the choices I faced in the wilderness outside the castle required me to decide either to fall back into an unconscious childlike limbo of passivity where my only concern was to meet the expectations of everyone else, or to grow into an adult who was discovering her own identity, developing her own potential, and taking control of her own life. In other words, I was trying to satisfy two basic conflicting needs in my life: my need for relationship and my need for individuation.

As I faced these forks in the road, I discovered that what separates the child from the adult is the recognition that we do not have to keep walking down the same rut-filled road we have traveled all our lives. We have choices. We can stop and look around. We can sit at a fork in the road and endure the agony of considering a new direction and the indecision of not knowing which way to go. And then when we are ready, we can choose to go our own way, in our own time.

12

Who Was Eve: Wanton or Wanderer?

ADAM AND EVE HAD EVERYTHING in the Garden of Eden, didn't they? Well, almost everything. They didn't have the knowledge of good and evil, but we are told that Eve and the snake changed that. God had given Adam and Eve only one rule: Do not eat the fruit from the Tree of Knowledge of Good and Evil. For a while, Adam and Eve found it easy to honor this rule, for there was much to discover in the beautiful garden and each other.

But eventually temptation came. In the Garden of Eden story, temptation is symbolized by a snake who suggested they break God's rule. At first Eve must have resisted, but gradually the forbidden fruit took on greater and greater significance in her mind until she became obsessed with it. How did it taste? she must have asked herself. What made that tree so special? And what was the big deal about taking a little bite of fruit? Why shouldn't they eat it? "C'mon, Eve. Just one bite," we can imagine the tiny voice in her mind saying. And so the first rule was broken, and Adam and Eve were forced to leave the beautiful walled garden. And they lost their blissful innocence forever.

Apart from its religious significance, I believe this simple story about the first two people has lasted from ancient times to the present because of a powerful psychological truth it conveys about human existence. Each of us is destined to reenact the same primal story in our own lives if we are to grow into awareness. Carl Jung said that embarking on the inner journey toward meaning and wholeness is the task of the second half of life. And this is the thing that brings us to the point of leaving the safety of the castle walls to follow the mysterious call of the Golden Bear: questioning and perhaps, like Eve, breaking some of the rules that have heretofore governed our lives. This must happen, because questioning is the only way to become aware that we have the power of choice; and choosing, with full knowledge of the consequences of our choices, is the one faculty that separates the pitiful, powerless puppet from the gloriously free, truly responsible individual.

As long as the "rules" (by which I mean the accepted do's and don't's, should's and shouldn't's, and attitudes and values of our family, religion, and social groups) remain unchallenged, we remain in a state of blind ignorance, congratulating ourselves for our goodness, never suspecting that the rules we are so proud of keeping might not be in our own best interest, or even that good for anyone else. Like the Pharisees in Jesus' time, we are convinced we are doing the right thing by conforming to all the written and unwritten rules of our social groups. What we do not realize is that it is not the *rightness* that makes keeping the rules so appealing to us; it is the *safeness.* By choosing to remain under the illusion of security provided by outer control — in other words, by choosing to remain behind the carefully constructed walls of our castles — we retain the approval of our groups and protect ourselves from the confusion and terror of following our mysterious inner impulses.

For many years blind conformity felt right to me. In fact, I tended to feel rather proud of myself because I was such a "good girl" and almost always kept the rules. What I didn't know about myself was that many of the rules were easy for me to keep because of the loving, trusting way in which I'd been brought up, and the only reason I hadn't broken some of the hard ones was that I was afraid. I had yet to learn that a rule that's never tested is like a war that's never fought: Nothing whatsoever is gained or lost.

So, after realizing that my goodness was only a way to remain safe, I no longer had any reason to be proud of myself. There is no virtue in keeping a rule that is easy to keep or that you are afraid to test, just as there is no reason for a puppet to be proud of the way it moves. A puppet moves the way the strings are pulled; a fearful, blindly obedient person does the same thing. Both are lifeless, unconscious creatures, responding to the movement of someone else's hands, moving to the beat of someone else's music. Unless, like Pinocchio, they become aware of their slavery and begin to rebel against their masters, they will never be real, free people. As long as I was unable to challenge rules that kept me from expressing my individuality, I was, like Pinocchio, childishly resentful and depressed, wondering why life was passing me by and what I could do to change things.

I wanted to change, but I didn't know how. Questioning the rules seemed very dangerous to me, as if to question the rules would be to challenge God. To break a "God-given" rule felt like a very serious thing, so it seemed better to comply and ignore the little temptations. In reality this was the worst thing I could have done, for each time I complied with a rule that felt uncomfortable, I became resentful. But feeling resentful did not fit the image I had of myself, so I forced my annoyance to hide in the darkness of my unconscious, where it grew and acquired a poisonous power that sapped my vital energy as I struggled to keep it hidden. If Eve had refused to acknowledge her inner temptation, the snake within her would have grown until it so dominated her nightly dreams and waking hours that it would have eventually destroyed her.

Eternity is a long time to spend trying to hold a powerful snake underground — or trying to ignore the compelling call of the Golden Bear.

As I became more conscious of my dissatisfied feelings, I began to see how they were related to the unwritten rules I'd always lived by. For example, as a young girl I had accepted the role of being a compliant, pleasant, passive female. But as my dissatisfaction emerged, I began to wonder about this choice. What was so awful about expressing my anger? Why did I have to keep my thoughts to myself when I disagreed with someone in authority? Who said my differing opinions were always wrong? Was my powerful need for space and time to be alone really so selfish? What was so awful about wanting to do something different from what other people wanted me to do? Who said other people's needs were more important than my own? Why should I spend the rest of my life trying to keep everyone else happy at my own expense?

As I unearthed rule after rule, I began to see how silly and unnecessary some of them were, and I got a glimpse of how much I had sacrificed to keep them. The pendulum began to swing to the other extreme: Self-sacrifice seemed ridiculous, and at times I felt so angry that I wanted to give up sacrificing altogether. I wanted to break the rules without a struggle, to say "To hell with everyone else" without caring what anyone thought or who got hurt. But, except for rare times when my anger erupted despite my careful control, I couldn't bring myself to indulge in wholesale rebellion, no matter how satisfying it might have felt! Rebellion is often chosen by people who have been badly hurt by their upbringing or who, like Pinocchio, are simply too innocent or ignorant to know any better; but I had been well-taught and well-loved. I cared too much about myself and my loved ones to be willing to suffer the nasty consequences I knew would result. No: Thoughtless, wanton rebellion was no more satisfactory a response to temptation than was total denial of its existence.

Then what was the best way to express these feelings?

Through sheer perseverance I gradually found the faint path that Eve long ago marked out for me and others like me. It is the way of the wanderer. It involves a conscious willingness to challenge the rules, which means leaving the safety of the castle and wandering in the wilderness while listening to the two opposing factions within oneself. One side (obedient Eve) wants to run back to the castle and keep the rules and stay safe; the other (rebellious snake) wants to follow the mysterious call of an inner traitor who urges us to treasonous acts against the rule of the realm.

Listening to both sides can be a very long, involved process lasting weeks, months, and even years; at times the inner chaos seems unbearable. We sense we may never find what we are looking for — we do not even know what we are looking for — yet neither can we give up. So we continue to wander in the wilderness, with no assurance that our quest will ever end.

To me, the important lesson to be learned from the story of Adam and Eve is a psychological and spiritual truth about the way we are all made: We begin in innocence and submit to the rules of our groups for as long as we need their support and protection. But when we are strong enough to become whole individuals, we will, like Eve, be tempted. And then we will have to wander all alone in a dark wilderness, searching for a path that is our own — neither conformity nor rebellion, but our own individual path to wholeness.

If God is omniscient, then God knew what would happen to Eve. Could it be that God wants us all, like Eve, to face our temptations honestly and suffer the agonies of becoming aware of the evil within us? Could it be that this is God's way of bringing us out of blind ignorance and slavery into moral responsibility and freedom? If this is so, then Eve was a courageous pioneer, not a miserable, wanton sinner. She is our psychological mother, the one who made humanity aware of its hope of attaining wholeness by leaving our walls behind and searching in the wilderness for the elusive, mysterious Golden Bear that calls us to consciousness.

As for me, I'm glad Eve took that bite!

13

Following the Golden Bear

AT THE AGE OF THIRTY-SEVEN, I had it all: a successful husband who loved me and whom I loved; two beautiful, healthy children; and a warm, comfortable home. I also had two exciting and prestigious part-time jobs. I was an adjunct instructor at a local university and the coordinator of children's programming at a television station. I had everything a woman could want.

Then why was I unhappy? Why indeed.

Why can't you just be happy? I would ask myself. I had no idea. I just knew that I yearned for something more, something I didn't understand. Something having to do with freedom. Sometimes I caught glimpses of it in certain books or movies, but I couldn't put my finger on it. Sometimes I sensed it late at night when I was alone with my thoughts in the dark. And sometimes

I heard a haunting call in music, and my eyes would fill with tears. I thought there must be something terribly wrong with me.

My husband was advancing rapidly in his career and seemed to grow in confidence and contentment every day. Maybe a return to a full-time, prestigious job was what I needed, too, I thought. I enjoyed the college classes I was teaching; I wondered if I would be happy as a full-time professor. So, with my husband's full support, I decided to get my doctoral degree.

And that's when things began to fall apart. I not only had the demands of my home and family and two jobs to consider, I also had college classes to attend. At first I thought I could handle the added responsibilities just as easily as I had always handled everything else. But this decision necessitated many changes in our lives that neither my husband nor I had foreseen. And I hadn't taken the contents of my unconscious into consideration. Dissatisfaction had been bubbling around in there for a long, long time, and it needed an outlet.

I, who had always been proud of my ability to sacrifice my own needs and be sweetly calm in even the most frustrating situations, could no longer contain my irritation. Situations and behaviors I had quietly accepted for years were growing to problems of major proportions, and molehills were turning into mountains. I was tired of pretending, tired of sacrificing, tired of letting everyone else call the shots. Naturally, this irritation resulted in some difficult confrontations with my husband. Secretly I began to believe that most of my discomfort was his fault, and he became the bad guy in my mind and the focus for my anger. The castle walls could no longer contain my feelings and needs, and they no longer fit my sense of self.

Then, after several months of mounting frustrations, a crisis occurred that shook me to the core of my being. For some, especially those without my kind of religious and ethical background, it would have been no more bothersome than the momentary buzzing of a mosquito. But for me it was the ultimate conflict, and it presented me with the most difficult decision of my life. I met a very attractive man and, against my conscious will, against every moral precept I had ever tried to follow, for the first time in my life I seriously considered having an affair.

I had never experienced a temptation so powerful and was deeply shocked at myself. Although the man lived in another town, we found ourselves in the same place a few times a month. In the time between, I thought obsessively of him. Part of me was able to stand outside and look at myself with stern objectivity. I was acting like a ridiculous child, I thought. I should be able to control my mind and my body. It was dangerous and stupid to indulge these feelings. I would simply have to use my willpower to keep this thing under control.

But the other part of me didn't want to keep it under control. I enjoyed this new feeling of being intensely alive. I liked being in the center of an exciting internal drama. I knew that if I allowed myself to act out my drama in the exterior world, it had the potential of turning into a tragedy, and that was the last thing I wanted. But I also realized that I wanted to give in to my temptation. The "bad" little girl — the naughty, instinctual creature who had been hiding behind the wall where it had been banished long ago by my "good" little girl — had grown into a powerful woman who was demanding at last to be part of my life.

I agonized over my conflict for six months. I had already cast off many of the bricks that made up my wall, but compared to this boulder, they were nothing but pebbles! I had left the castle and wandered in the wilderness, making many difficult choices to follow the Golden Bear, but this fork in the road was totally unlike any of the others. This was the big one.

I could see no right answer, no way out. I began to have difficulty sleeping, and my stomach bothered me so much that I couldn't eat and I lost twenty pounds. I was filled with fear and dread, for it seemed to me that the battle raging within me was between God and the devil.

When it came to this issue, my traditional religious beliefs were not easily discarded like so many used bricks. I was certain that God would want me to return to the castle; that meant that the Golden Bear was the devil. The idea of following the devil was unthinkable, yet the inner demands of this "devil" were so powerfully compelling that I felt it would be a dreadful mistake to ignore them. This meant I had to challenge God, or at least my interpretation of God. This crisis was showing me that my old morality based on conformity and safety didn't work anymore. I was going to have to develop a new one that did.

And so I began to examine closely the moral beliefs I had always taken for granted, especially the ones about female sexuality. For example, I'd always assumed I had done the right thing in conforming to the double standard and repressing my sexuality as a teen-age girl. But, with these feelings reawakened, I was beginning to see female sexuality as truly beautiful. My body was telling me something very different from the rules my mind had always followed.

In light of these emerging feelings, I saw the sexual double standard of my youth as primarily a way by which men who were afraid of women's sexuality tried to control it. I also questioned the biblical commandment against adultery. What made adultery so bad? Was there something inherently wrong about the sex act itself when it was not sanctioned by marital vows, as I had always assumed? Or was the real evil in the terrible damage adultery often caused, especially to trusting spouses and innocent children? Was the reason I'd never seriously considered having an affair before because I was a person of great integrity and high moral standards? Or could it be that I was appalled at the idea of breaking this rule simply because I was afraid — afraid of being punished by God, afraid of what people would think?

Suddenly I saw that fearing the judgment of my society and the God it had taught me to believe in was a pretty flimsy foundation for ethical behavior. I began to evaluate my moral dilemma in new terms that neither condemned my true feelings nor mindlessly accepted collective assumptions about God. I was developing a new concept of God as a loving parent who respected me as an individual and considered my needs important, not someone who wanted me to follow the rules just because they were the rules. From now on, it was this God who would have authority over me. After God, I would consider my own needs to be as important as those of others: I would be equal. This meant I would have to be totally honest with myself and others; and, since equality is reciprocal, it meant I would have to care about protecting others from needless pain as much as I had always cared about protecting myself.

Soon, this man and I acknowledged our attraction to each other. The choice, which until this point had only been theoretical, became real. I realized I no longer wanted to make the decision my friends, my family, or my ancestors would have insisted I make. For the first time in my life, I saw that I had my own choice. I could do the reasonable, sensible thing and continue to be the obedient, passionless puppet who never rocked the boat, i.e., I could continue to live my life according to the principle of rational Logos. Or I could believe that God cared more about what was best for me, an individual, than about my conformity to a group. I could be true to my Self and live with vitality and passion. In other words, I could accept the nonrational demands of the feminine principle of Eros, the way of instinct, emotion, and deep involvement in life.

One night as I lay in bed struggling with this issue as I did every night, I simply felt a sudden clarity and sense of peace about choosing to be true to myself despite all opposition. I decided to have an affair. I thought this probably went against the "will of God," as I had understood God most of my life, and that I might be punished either in this life or the next. I knew my decision might hurt some people, although I was determined to do everything possible to keep this from happening. But I also knew that despite all the obvious reasons against it, this choice affirmed my needs and my life and my right to live it in my own way and to make my own mistakes. It was a choice to leave the fog of apathy and enter into the fullness of my life with passion. It was a choice for life and, although I felt I was being torn apart, it was a choice for wholeness.

That night I prayed more fervently and sincerely than I'd ever prayed before. I confessed to God that I was no longer willing to be a passive victim, always tossed about by the choices of everyone else and then blaming them for my unhappiness. I admitted that my choice might be "wrong," but I was making it anyway. I said I would accept full responsibility for the consequences. And, in one last cry for help, out of the depths of my profound trust in the superiority of God's wisdom and love for me, I gave God permission to do anything He (I still thought of God in masculine terms then) needed to do to stop me if it was His will. But I told Him that if He didn't stop me, I was going through with it. This decision took more courage than anything I'd ever done, and I was very frightened. But after that night I felt more hopeful and alive than I had in years.

The next day I called the man and told him of my decision. We made plans to meet two weeks later. Moments after making the call, I put my right hand into the pocket of the navy blue blazer I was wearing and felt a slip of paper. I pulled it out and read it. It said, "Because thou hast kept the word of my patience, I will also keep thee from the hour of temptation" (Rev. 3:10).

It was a Bible verse one of my children had given me after Sunday School months before. I had slipped it into my pocket and forgotten about it. I gaped at this message in disbelief and amazement. Wave after wave of hot chills washed up the back of my neck to the top of my head. With grim determination I defiantly challenged God. "All right, God," I said aloud. "Go right ahead and stop me if You want to and if You think You can. I gave You permission and I meant it. But I haven't changed my mind." And I put the slip of paper back into my pocket.

When we met two weeks later, my friend said he had decided not to have an affair with me. He gave me many logical reasons why he simply couldn't go through with it at this time. My temptation was removed, and I no longer had any choice in the matter.

My six months of wandering in a dangerous, chaotic wilderness had apparently been for nothing. I felt as if I were the victim of a cruel joke, as if a rug had been viciously yanked out from under my feet. All my life I had been the best little girl I could possibly be so that I would stay safe. But the wicked little child behind my wall had sabotaged me. She had convinced me to drop my defenses and follow the Golden Bear into the wilderness of unlimited choice and dangerous risk. She had tricked me into seeing and hearing and feeling something real that came from inside of me, and the moment I allowed myself to be truly vulnerable, the moment I approached the turbulent river of life once again where I dared to hope I might obtain the beautiful red rose, the moment I felt alive again as I had once felt as a little child — I was run over by a steamroller.

As painful as this experience was, it was the catalyst that forced me to grow at last. In making my decision to break with my habitual behavior, I broke a tie to a way of life I could never return to. I had answered a call to leave the castle and follow the Golden Bear, and the lily-white princess-child I had tried so hard to be was gone forever.

I had truly left the castle, but for me, the leaving never involved a physical separation, as it does for others. Somehow, I knew instinctively that the way to end my suffering and find the answers for my life did not lie in the outer world. I knew my discomfort was not really the fault of my husband. I knew nothing would be solved by leaving this good man and looking for another to take his place as the masculine authority in my life.

No, looking for the perfect man was not the answer for me, for, in truth, there was no such man in the outer world. He was only a dream, only my inner ideal, and it would be fruitless to search for him. I knew at last that it was unfair to expect my partner to make me perfectly happy. No man could ever replace the father-king I had idolized in my blissful childhood castle. No one knew how to make me safe and happy but me!

It was time to find my inner island where I would seek honest intimacy with the partner who loved me and whom I loved, instead of hiding behind walls or trying to escape the suffering this difficult task would entail. It was time to learn to stop expecting the men in my life to be gods and allow them to be human. It was time to find my own masculine authority — my soul mate, my hero, my Beloved — within.

Although I didn't know it yet, it was time to rescue my smothered femininity, to learn how to breathe like a queen who could rule her own life instead of abdicating her birthright and surrendering her rightful power. It was time to become a woman who appreciated her feminine strength, sexuality, passion, earthiness, mystery, instincts, and Eros capacity for true caring and compassion. It was time to recapture the feminine soul I had betrayed so long ago when I had decided to conform to the myth about a world where women have to be lily-white and only men can be heroes.

It was time to discover my Self, to find my true potential in all its masculine and feminine strengths, and to make peace with all that I truly was, whether it was valued by the world or not.

We each have a whole, inner Self that is the regulating center of our personalities. Becoming aware of it and learning to be true to it in our everyday lives is our destiny. This Self, written with a capital S to differentiate it from our much smaller, narrower conscious self, is experienced as a power greater than our egos: We experience this Self as a manifestation of God. If we get so caught up in living according to inflexible, collectively acceptable ways that we refuse to listen to our inner Self, this Self will demand to be heard — sometimes by bringing some of us, without our conscious awareness, to the point of crisis so we can no longer refuse to listen.

My refusal to listen to my Self had forced me into a crisis that seemed to have no solution. No matter which choice I made, it would have felt wrong to me. This situation caused terrible suffering that compelled me to take the demands of my inner Self seriously at last. I thought the choice was between remaining faithful to my husband and succumbing to the attraction of another man. But the real choice was between either continuing in my safe role of sacrificing everything for relationships or being true to my Self, who was nothing like the miserable puppet I had become.

By facing my temptation, I was forced at last to recognize my capacity for "evil." Perhaps I was capable of breaking a moral law I had always held sacred, but that didn't mean I was evil through and through. Perhaps it just meant I was forgivably human. When I began to understand this, when I could finally admit that the good little girl could be bad, when I was able to choose to honor this darker side of my personality instead of struggling to ignore and repress it, an amazing thing happened: The problem I could not solve was solved by a manifestation of God.

If I had stubbornly refused to consider the reality of my true Self and had continued to live only for outer relationships after this crisis, I think I would have been eaten up with remorse at my unlived life and eventually ended up a miserable, bitter woman. On the other hand, if I had chosen to honor an ethic of self-interest and irresponsibility, I would undoubtedly have done grave damage to both myself and my family. But because I suffered patiently until I could work out a new ethic that at last recognized my own authority while at the same time honored God's authority over me, I was not punished for my rebellion and I caused no damage to anyone, although the potential for harm was great indeed. I was, instead, delivered from my temptation.

The Golden Bear was not the devil. I had gotten it backward! It was my resistance to accepting myself as I was and developing my God-given potential that was the devil. The Golden Bear was that manifestation of God within me, the Self that knew I was ready to face my temptation all alone in that dark island abyss at the center of my being instead of looking for ways to escape my destiny of self-confrontation. It was God who led me away from the safety of conformity to the edge of the terrible, turbulent river of life. It was God who gave me the strength to enter it. And there was no going back. My eyes had been opened, and I knew at last that I had not only the power but the right to live my own life and make my own decisions. I was changed for eternity, never to be an innocent little princess again.

This was when God ceased to be an idea to me. This was when I learned that some kinds of suffering are holy and that God is a living, loving reality. And this was when I finally knew that I would never find wholeness in doctrines and authorities in the outside world. It was time to listen carefully to my own heart, to the divine spark of life that blazed within me. It was time to find the only destiny that could ever satisfy me: my very own.

PART THREE
A Time for Dying

14

Perfection, or Who's the Purest of Them All?

OUR ISLAND WORK USUALLY BEGINS when our psychic pain is so intense that we are forced to acknowledge our need for help. For most people, counseling or therapy is by far the most efficient means of getting help. It is unnecessarily difficult to proceed without guidance from a trained professional because the obstacles to growth are so powerful and pervasive.

Some of these obstacles are fear, apathy, laziness, and lack of motivation. One of the strongest is the unconscious desire to escape the pain of this difficult work by such means as sleeping too much, watching too much television, becoming addicted to alcohol or drugs, procrastinating, or keeping so busy that one never finds time for inner work. A good therapist can help in overcoming these obstacles.

There have always been a few people who have insisted on proceeding on their own, however. This is the more difficult way, but it is possible. In my own case, I went two or three times to my priest for counseling, and occasionally unburdened myself a little to a few trusted friends. But most of my work was done alone. Fortunately, I've always been a seeker, and my need for healing and understanding was very powerful; and so, through trial and error, I discovered the resources I needed to find some of my own answers.

My major resources were spiritual and intellectual. My faith in the truth of the teachings of Jesus and my belief in a God who loved me for myself led me to a great deal of praying and meditating. My meditating was never formal. It just came naturally to me to spend at least an hour every day of focused, introspective thinking about certain issues or problems. As I look back on it now, I realize that I always approached problems from two perspectives: I would try to figure out how God would want me to think or act on this problem, and I would try to get in touch with my true feelings about it. Then, if there was any conflict between the two, I would try to resolve it.

This inner contemplation could happen at any time of the day, but my two favorite times were on the long drive to and from work and just before I fell asleep at night. Often it took the form of an imaginary conversation with a friend or supposed antagonist in which I would try to persuade him or her to see my point of view. In other words, I talked to myself!

My other major resource was intellectual. I've always loved learning from books, so during this period I read widely, especially in the areas of psychological and spiritual growth.

Through spiritually-oriented introspection and reading, I discovered seven ways of getting in touch with the obscure inhabitants of my island. They are:

- Noticing the things I dislike most about other people
- Becoming more aware of my real feelings and emotions
- Paying attention to clues from my body

- Facing my fear of death and allowing myself to grieve
- Creative work (writing poetry worked best for me)
- Recording and analyzing my dreams
- Making a conscious effort to understand and value my own femininity and the feminine aspect of God

My island experience was a very painful time when I felt as if many old aspects of myself were dying, and these tools taught me much about my Self.

The island is the realm of the Self, the regulating center of our personalities. That world encompasses everything about us, the good and the bad, our entire potential, our divine essence — everything. Our sojourn on the island is the time to face these things with brutal honesty. We must discard the false images of ourselves that our childish egos have cherished and make peace with the truth. We must sort out and examine each negative thought, every selfish motive. Slowly, step by step, our fearful childlike egos must die so that our negative parts can be modified and integrated in a nondestructive way into the real, whole, mature Self that is struggling to be born into our conscious lives. The work is slow and difficult and never completely finished.

"What?" you say. "You mean I have to accept the bad parts of myself? No way! You must be crazy. I'm not giving in to laziness, lust, selfishness, fear, and greed. I have spent a lifetime trying to be perfect. Now you say I have to stop? Didn't Jesus say, 'Be ye therefore perfect, even as your Father which is in heaven is perfect' (Matt. 5:48)? Well, that's all I'm trying to be: perfect!"

I'll illustrate what I mean by taking a look at Snow White.

Don't you just love Snow White? She was about as close to perfect as a person can be. White as snow. Lily white. White as light. Loving, generous, forgiving, tactful. She had good manners, a good attitude. She was very polite and always smiling. Her hair was always clean and shiny. Her clothes were neat. I'll bet she smelled great! Gosh, was she pure! Every mother's dream. Wouldn't you love to have a kid like that?

With all that perfection, why did Snow White have so many problems? What was the point of the nasty, vain stepmother? Why couldn't whoever made up that story leave well enough alone?

Here is why. For the same reason a seesaw does not work if you only sit on one end. For the same reason it is not summer all year long. Or light for twenty-four hours a day.

Not clear yet? For the same reason Jim Bakker and Jimmy Swaggart fell off their electronic altars. For the same reason the purest Puritans persecuted a plethora of witches. Or the primmest Victorians led underground sex lives that rivaled the most pagan bacchanalian revels.

And for the same reason our planet is clutching her poisoned entrails and gasping for breath under a darkening cloud of noxious gases. For the same reason life form after life form is being snuffed out for eternity. For the same reason righteous officials send armies of innocents and religious leaders send armies of infidels to slaughter and be slaughtered.

The reason? One-sidedness. That's all. All these situations came about because someone believed that as long as they followed one image of perfection, nothing could go wrong. Many of them broke under the load of that one-sided perfection, and their other, dark side came exploding out.

But one-sidedness does not work, because it is anti-nature, anti-God, anti-life. Because perfection cannot be found in one-sidedness of any kind: not absolute goodness, not perfect reason, not spotless purity. Then what in heaven's name did Jesus mean when he said we should be perfect?

The word *perfect* has more than one meaning. The way Jesus used it, perfect means completed, or whole. It does not mean always good, or spotlessly pure. And here is the paradox that we find so difficult to accept: In order to be truly whole, we have to be honest with ourselves, and this means acknowledging those things within us that we think of as bad as well as those we consider good.

Humans are made up of both mind and body, but Western

society has been profoundly influenced by first Greek and then Christian thought, both of which give the mind much more recognition. Like the ancient Greeks, who believed in the inherent superiority of Logos over Eros, we have come to believe that the "lower" physical, bodily aspect of our nature is inferior to the "higher" intellectual, spiritual one. This conviction has led scholars and religious leaders to teach us to suspect and even hate our physical selves.

Unfortunately, it is a law of nature that any time we disturb the delicate balance between naturally occurring opposites by giving preference to one over the other, we are asking for trouble. Thus, for example, when we insist on the superiority of the human mind over nature and think we can control natural forces instead of respecting their unique claims and coexisting peacefully with them, we cause terrible problems for ourselves, destroying the very earth we must live on. In other words, our distorted emphasis on mind over matter, or masculine/Logos over feminine/Eros, is killing us.

There is no way we can achieve perfection by accepting only half our nature. By seeking only cerebral purity, we deny an essential component of our humanness. By identifying solely with reason and logic, we cut off our capacity for passion, intuition, instinct, and feelings. By relating exclusively to a pure, disembodied spirit, we neglect our very real, natural, physical human demands and call them bad. And, in the name of reason and perfection, we start finger-pointing, name-calling, wall-building, and war-mongering.

Most of us are only able to face those things we have always thought of as imperfections when the circumstances in our lives become so unbearable that we no longer have the energy to pretend. I was convinced I could handle anything until the strains and pressures of college and two jobs severely tested my capacity to be the perfect wife and mother. And then I was confronted with the crisis that took away the rest of my resistance. In my weariness I had to wonder why I was so obsessed with perfection. Maintaining my well-constructed disguise took all my energy, and I was no happier for all the effort. I thought it would be such a relief to stop trying so hard and simply be myself.

I was tired of wearing Snow White's smile. Tentatively, a little at a time, I began to risk peeling it off to see what was underneath. This is when my island work began.

Island work is not for the faint-hearted. Like Christine, the innocent young singer who earnestly persuaded the Phantom of the Opera to take off his mask, we may be painfully convinced of our puny audacity in challenging the masters and mistresses of our unconscious, and we may faint at our first sight of the ugliness. But it is only when the ugliness has been unmasked and we can see it for what it truly is that it loses its negative power over us and we can begin to learn from it.

The Phantom was certainly a dark and frightening creature, but behind that hideous face was a pure musical soul with the voice of an angel. If Christine had refused to grant that masculine soul and voice their rightful place in her life, she would never have achieved her destiny. Instead of rejecting the Phantom for his ugliness, she came to love him, and in the final act of lifting the mask a second time and kissing his grotesque face, she rescued her own soul.

Snow White had the same problem. She was tormented again and again by her wicked stepmother, a dark, vain, and passionate feminine antagonist — psychologically the opposite, shadow side of Snow White's own conscious personality — who did everything she could to destroy the sweet passive child who knew nothing of evil. Snow White's trials were long and painful, but by patiently enduring them she was brought to the point where she could awaken to her masculine strengths (represented by the kiss of the prince), conquer her own evil tendencies (represented by her wicked stepmother), gain enough balance to stand on her own two feet, become a mature woman, and marry her prince.

Like Christine and Snow White, I had to pay attention to what the dark, unknown things in my own unconscious — both the hideous masculine phantom and the wicked feminine step-mother — were teaching me. It was not easy to stop blaming others and admit to my own hurt, anger, thoughtlessness, dishonesty, selfishness, sensitivity, and pride. But I knew I had to face the truth about myself if I was ever to live in peace with myself.

As long as we are caught up in a pursuit of lily-white purity, we will not understand that it can be good to acknowledge our imperfections. It sounds very dangerous, like condoning selfishness or affirming anarchy. But that, of course, is not what I mean. I mean that it is essential for the welfare of our souls that we move from a state of unconsciousness in which we refuse to see our own flaws, into a state of awareness in which we accept ourselves in our rosy-red entirety.

In my quest to uncover my flaws, it helped me to think of the negative, or troublesome, aspects of my personality as individual characters living in my unconscious. Most of us think of ourselves as only one character, the one we call by our own name. This is our ego, the conscious part of us that thinks, acts, and makes decisions. But humans have both a conscious and an unconscious life. Sometimes we act in ways that we do not really want to, or say things we did not consciously mean to say, or sense that we are many different people, depending on the situation. That is because within each of us there is a cast of widely varied characters, male and female, each with different needs and goals; and all of them are legitimate aspects of our truest, fullest Selves.

We are consciously aware of some of these characters, like the responsible mother or the supportive spouse or the dedicated worker, but many of the other characters within us, like the critical judge or the abandoned orphan or the self-pitying victim, are hidden in the unconscious where we cannot see them. Every single character within us is an important, potentially helpful part of our personality. If the audience (our conscious self) pays attention to a character and listens to its lines, that character will gladly take its appropriate role in the play, neither hogging center stage nor sulking in the wings.

But if we refuse to acknowledge some players because we fear or disapprove of them, they will resent our neglect and seek our attention by disrupting the play in uncomfortable ways. Because we do not even know they exist, they can have tremendous negative power over us. They can cause irrational fears, terrible nightmares, outbursts of temper, compulsive behaviors, personality disorders, and even physical ailments. The more they are resisted, the more powerful and destructive they become.

The trick, of course, is to find these hidden characters and allow them to perform the parts they have been given without ruining the play. One way I've found to get in touch with my personal cast of inner players is to pay attention to the things I most dislike in others.

We are overly critical of certain qualities in others because we fear and hate these same qualities in ourselves. If we are especially critical of laziness in others, for example, it is because deep within ourselves we suspect we have a tendency to be lazy. But because we do not want to be lazy or admit that we sometimes are, we deny it in ourselves and are acutely sensitive to it in others.

Here is an example of how becoming aware of my criticism of others worked for me. At a very young age I decided (unconsciously, of course) that if I could be perfect I would be safe. I thought a "perfect" person must always be in control of her emotions, especially anger. So, being a perfect person, I could never be angry.

For a long time I was able to contain my anger, and I felt superior to others who couldn't. In fact, the thing that annoyed me most about my husband was that sometimes he couldn't control his anger. That should have given me a clue that anger was really my problem, but it didn't. I could never see my own anger, only everyone else's. As a result, much of my work on the island was about anger. Even now that I can admit to being angry, I still usually justify it by blaming the other person for being angry first!

Noticing my own pet peeves, or the things I most dislike in others, has helped me to discover the angry woman and other undesirable characters inside myself. When I first started looking at myself this way, I found it extremely difficult to believe that the things I disliked most in others were really in myself. But the more attention I paid to the motives that underlay my words and behaviors, the more capable I became of accepting painful truths about myself.

I no longer believe that humans can be perfected. But it is possible for us to become more aware, and thus gain greater control, of our imperfections. It is a strange paradox that only by allowing ourselves to be humanly imperfect are we able to move ourselves, and the world, a little closer to our enduring ideal of spiritual perfection, or salvation.

In the masculine hero myth, the hero kills his dragons, or inner and outer enemies, thereby earning his way to salvation. It is true that death always precedes transformation and rebirth, but the feminine way is not to fight perceived imperfections in order to destroy them. Rather, it is a peaceful way of withdrawing, contemplating, grieving, connecting, integrating, and accepting.

In our new feminine myth, the island is where this death of the old occurs; but not by means of a ferocious attack conducted by fearful egos who wish to conquer and destroy. It comes about gradually and naturally, through a diligent desire to allow the old to die a natural death in order to make way for the new, the way flowers fade and wilt after they have produced seeds from which new growth will arise in the spring. Making peace with our imperfections, allowing our outmoded limitations to grow old and die, is the work of the island — the alternative to dragon-slaying, the feminine way to salvation.

15

My Friend the Cougar

TRAINING MYSELF TO SEE THE CONNECTION between the annoying flaws of others and my own faults was probably the first task I began to master in the death stage of my journey. From there, it was only a short step to my next task: to become more aware of my real feelings and emotions.

The island task of recognizing my emotions entailed the hard work of looking past the image I tried to show the world and paying attention to what I was really feeling inside instead of how I was acting on the outside. I had always tried hard to be a sensitive, caring, understanding person, but I had to accept the painful truth that I did not always feel as nice as I acted. This was an important clue to some of the more obscure inhabitants of my island.

For example, there is a part of me that often feels critical of myself and others for having moral flaws and character defects such as weakness, laziness, carelessness, thoughtlessness, or selfishness. It helped me to see this aspect of my personality as a powerful, stoic, Self-Righteous Puritan. This humorless inner ascetic firmly believes in rising above personal discomfort and never complaining. She abhors pride, self-pity, and excuses. Sometimes she feels very self-important and superior to me and others who are weaker and less capable than she is. Because these critical feelings are so abhorrent to my conscious self, it took me a long time to recognize this aspect of my personality.

This character has appeared many times in my dreams as a powerful, aggressive woman. Once she was a tall, intense, dark-haired woman in an aerobics outfit who was exercising intently by the side of the road. When I tried to get past her, she barred my way. Once she was a stern old lady who was trying to make a little boy feel guilty about enjoying himself too much in anticipation of Christmas. And once she was a cruel Russian policewoman who was preparing to punish me for helping a boy escape from prison. What I learned on the island is that she is just as much a part of me as the much nicer person I generally show the outside world, and I've learned to recognize her presence in the negative, judgmental, tough-minded feelings I sometimes have toward myself and others.

Another of my inner characters is a self-pitying orphan who used to feel very inadequate and inferior. She desperately wanted to please the Self-Righteous Puritan, but for years she rarely succeeded. As a result she often felt resentful and disheartened. Sometimes she felt depressed. This Hard-Working Orphan has also appeared in my dreams in various roles, such as a talented trapeze artist whom no one noticed, an insecure hotel maid, or an unappreciated secretary.

A third emotional inhabitant of my island kingdom was harder to recognize. Perhaps that is because she is much lower on the evolutionary scale than the Self-Righteous Puritan or the

Hard-Working Orphan. She is, in fact, an instinctual, primitive four-legged creature: a large, angry feline.

I've already mentioned my struggle with anger. One of my most difficult tasks on the island was to see and accept this despised emotion within myself. I grew up in a conservative family that was embarrassed by strong feelings and emotions, and we were all proud of our genteel restraint. During my early adulthood, when I got married and took my first teaching job, I continued to think that expressing anger was unnecessary and vulgar. Secretly, I congratulated myself on being free from such an ugly emotion. In retrospect I can see that there were many occasions when anger would have been perfectly justifiable and when I must certainly have felt it. But because it did not fit my image of myself, I refused to acknowledge it.

I think my inability to admit my anger was partly due to a lack of self-esteem, partly a characteristic of my native personality, and partly the result of strong conditioning by a society that considers women's anger to be proof of their emotional inferiority and tendency toward bitchiness! I believed that emotionalism was a negative "feminine" trait and that anger was bad. I thought that if I couldn't control my emotions, especially anger, someone might think I was bad — as, indeed, I secretly suspected.

It was not until the birth of my second child that I began to suspect that I might not be able to keep this up forever. I realized that I didn't fit easily into the traditional role I had assigned myself of perfect compliant wife, perfect patient mother, and perfect immaculate housekeeper. I felt vague stirrings of frustration about being stuck in a role that was simply not fulfilling many of my needs. I began to see that I was hiding some angry feelings in order to keep peace and appear to be calm and under control.

Naturally, when I began to suspect this, the burden of guilt was unendurable. In my desire to be superwoman it seemed totally unacceptable to question my role or even *feel* anger, let alone express it, and each time I did so I thought I was flawed, selfish, and self-indulgent. The result was that I usually held it in until I could no longer contain it. Then, once or twice a year when I felt pushed to my absolute limits, a volcanic explosion of primitive, goddess-like rage would burst forth.

My anger also came out in my dreams. As a new mother I once dreamed that a fierce tiger was trying to come into my house through a sliding glass door to get my baby who was sleeping just inside. This was a tiger to be afraid of — and I was — but I bravely stood between it and my baby, ready to defend her to the death. If someone had told me then that this tiger represented my own anger at my lovely child for all the sacrifices her existence was forcing upon me, I wouldn't have believed it. I was too busy convincing myself that I was in control of this motherhood thing, just as I had always been in control of every other aspect of my life. But there was a part of me that was angry then, and I was deeply afraid of this dangerous creature within me. Who knew what it was capable of doing if released?

Finally, during the island phase of my journey, I began to stop denying my anger. It was time to make peace with it. I began to understand that anger is a natural human emotion, not a shameful sign of weakness. Once I started believing this, I stopped judging myself for being that lowest of all human creatures: an emotional female! And as I learned to like myself better, I lost the need to hide my feelings from others, for I no longer feared their judgment or thought their opinions of me were more correct or important than my own.

When I faced my anger, it stopped appearing in my dreams as an enemy. For example, one night I allowed myself to be angry and I single-handedly punched out three adult men who were beating up my son! And twice I dreamed of a lovely pet cougar. Once it walked beside me on the sidewalk and snarled at some men who appeared threatening. Another time it rode with me in the back seat of my car. I knew it was dangerous, but I also knew it was my friend and under my control.

Over the years my efforts to notice my true feelings have paid off. When I become aware of critical feelings, I no longer think I must be a terrible person. I simply acknowledge that my overly strict, Self-Righteous Puritan has arrived on the scene. She seems content to be recognized, and no longer succeeds in wounding me and others as much as she used to.

When I feel myself becoming hurt or resentful, I realize that the Hard-Working Orphan is feeling inadequate and unappreciated. Perhaps I've been struggling hard to do something difficult and I need some encouragement or a pat on the back. Instead of pouting because no one notices, I simply tell the truth about what I'm doing and how hard it is. That way I get the help, encouragement, or attention I need.

And when I sense the approach of the cougar, I let her growl a little right away before she becomes so worked up that she has to roar. It is amazing how simple and painless this is. Treated this way, anger is no longer a mysterious evil threat; it is a life-affirming, liberating release.

During the island phase of my journey, I came to understand that if I'm to be a complete human being, I must accept all my inner dragons; that is the major component of island work. I know there are still some dragons in there that I haven't gotten up the nerve to face yet, but somehow I'm not as afraid of them as I used to be. I guess that's because I've experienced such an exhilarating sense of accomplishment each time I've made peace with one of them. There are times when even anger is not a dangerous beast, but a helpful friend.

16

Messages from My Body

AN IMPORTANT LESSON I LEARNED on the island was to pay attention to messages from my body. Our bodies have a language all their own and they do not lie. This is the principle behind the lie detector. We can be saying one thing, but the detector picks up subtle changes in our body temperature, pulse rate, and breathing that indicate quite a different version.

Some body language is a result of our conscious awareness. For example, if I want to show someone that I'm willing to listen to what they have to say, I sit quietly and look attentively at them.

But much of the body's language is an expression of what is going on in the unconscious mind. For instance, even though I may be deliberately giving my attention to someone who is speaking, if my arms and legs are crossed, my teeth are clenched, my stomach is starting to hurt, there is a dull pain in my temples, and my facial muscles are very firm and tight, these are signals from my unconscious that I'm feeling stubbornly resistant to this person and his or her words.

When I notice any tension or discomfort in my body, it helps to ask myself what inner character is causing this reaction. I imagine who this is, and what he or she is trying to tell me.

Suppose I'm talking to a difficult relative. Even though I've always been nice to her, she cuts me down behind my back. I realize she is a bitter, unhappy person, so I've made a conscious effort to forgive and accept her without taking her cruelty personally. But here I am, listening to her problems compassionately, with clenched teeth, an uncomfortable feeling in the pit of my stomach, and the beginnings of a whale of a headache.

What inner character is sending out such powerful signals? It is certainly not the mature, understanding adult I've tried so hard to be. Somewhere inside me there is an angry, wounded child, thrashing out at the injustice of having to be nice to this nasty bully who has caused me such pain. It will do no good to ignore this child. The physical symptoms will not go away until I acknowledge the wounded child's presence and deal honestly with its (my) anger.

I might do this by openly confronting the person who arouses these feelings, or I might resolve to be more honest with him or her in the future. Facing this truth might mean writing down my angry feelings, or talking about them with a third person, or any number of other things. The important thing is that I've learned to become aware of my true feelings and find some way of expressing them so my body doesn't have to bear the burden.

Our bodies, like our pet peeves and innermost feelings, are vehicles that carry important messages from our unconscious selves to our struggling, confused conscious selves. It is far easier to ignore these subtle messages than to take the time to notice and respond to them, but we do so at considerable cost to our mental and physical health. The result can be the appearance of various mental disturbances, including uncontrollable anxieties and phobias. Physically, we may experience uncomfortable and, in extreme cases, life-threatening disturbances that suggest, with striking symbology, the nature of the unconscious problem.

It is not uncommon for a person who "bends over backward" or "breaks her back" for others to have back problems. Similarly, someone who stubbornly and blindly refuses to expand her narrow-minded vision or see her own faults can develop unusual visual symptoms. A person who tries to rationalize his anger by blaming it on others, or who tries to talk himself out of it at an intellectual level instead of honestly expressing it, might develop severe headaches. Someone who carries the "weight of the world," assuming all the responsibilities for everyone else at home or at work, might suffer from a painful shoulder. A rigid, self-righteous person might develop a stiff neck or back. And a person who continually denies her emotional pain might be riddled with bodily pains for which no physical cause or remedy can be found.

Of course, not all physical problems are caused by our refusal to see ourselves honestly, but many of them are. For this reason, any time I have an uncomfortable physical symptom, I look for an inner mental attitude that seems to be related to it.

For example, at the beginning of my island stay, my body showed me the rigidity of the Self-Righteous Puritan by treating me to an annoying stiff neck that lasted for three or four days. At the time, I didn't get the message, and I continued to expect stiff, wooden, morally correct attitudes from myself and others. Amazingly, since I've learned to relax and see the Self-Righteous Puritan in my behavior, I've stopped having stiff necks.

The Hard-Working Orphan seems to have two favorite communication tools. One is my stomach. Whenever I get a stomachache, I can be sure she has been working too hard to do something she doesn't really like. This happens especially in relationships.

Once I was talking with a person who seemed to have a hidden agenda of manipulation and control. Outwardly she was extremely warm and friendly, but something about her manner toward me felt very dishonest. I wanted to like her and I tried hard to accept her, telling myself that everyone has problems and she was no worse than anyone else. But by the time we parted, my stomach hurt. It took three stomachaches before I realized that I just couldn't stomach that woman!

My Hard-Working Orphan also gets to me through my eyes. On four occasions I've had what the doctor called ocular migraines. The pain from these was never more than a dull thud at the back of my head, so it was easy to ignore. But when gray patches blocked out more and more of my sight, and flashing lights began to appear at the corners of my visual field, I was forced to stop what I was doing. Every time this happened, I was hard at work at a task I either disliked or was too tired to enjoy anymore. My body was showing me that I was stressing myself out; it was time to stop, to close my eyes and rest. As soon as I responded, the migraine went away.

The angry feline often attacks my head. For me, a headache is a pretty good indication that I'm angry, or at least frustrated or annoyed.

Before my island experience, I thought only my head knew who I really was and what I ought to do, even though my body told me otherwise in very graphic language. Our bodies, like the body of our Mother Earth, are very resilient. But they are also very sensitive to extremes. They need balance and tender care, and if we do not respect these needs, our bodies become, like this planet, dangerously fragile. We refuse to heed their impassioned messages at our peril.

17

Fear of Dying

THERE IS NO WAY TO AVOID DEATH on the journey to whole-ness. It has to be confronted when we withdraw to the island. It comes with the territory. The island is the place at the very center of our being where we finally face our greatest fears. Only by facing these things can we discover new sources of hope.

Dying is a subject most of us prefer not to talk about. Yet, we all think about it — sometimes more than we would like to. I believe that if we could bring ourselves to deal with dying and death more directly, we would find it easier to come to grips with our fears. For that reason I would like to share a few of my experiences. When we share our own stories, we find there are far more people than we expected who have had similar experiences and for whom the sharing is affirming, enlightening, and reassuring.

Until I experienced the crisis that took me to the island, I rarely thought about death. Even when I did, it was fairly easy to forget it again. But once I got to the island, I could no longer avoid the subject. By choosing to create a new life instead of conforming to the old one, I had given my old, childish, safety-obsessed ego permission to die. Moreover, I had set myself up for a totally unknown, frightening future. Inside I was in deep mourning for the loss of my familiar crutches, and I was profoundly fearful that I would never find anything better to replace them. But although I was suffering acutely within, in the outside world I continued to function normally.

I'm not a hypochondriac who runs to a doctor every few months with imaginary illnesses. In fact, I've gone for years at a time without seeing a doctor of any kind. But there were a few times during this island period when, with very little provocation, I was convinced that I was going to die, when I thought my death must be imminent. At these times I either superstitiously interpreted a few coincidental occurrences or images as prophetic omens, or I became obsessed with a minor symptom or two that would normally seem inconsequential but which I blew up all out of proportion until I was certain the end was near.

For example, when I was getting my doctorate, near the middle of one semester I noticed a slight, odd-shaped rash on my face, and I began to dwell upon it until I was convinced it was terminal. I was sure I had lupus or another disease that features a rash. After seeing a doctor, I realized that the rash was caused by the solution from my contact lenses. I started drying my fingers before touching my face, and the rash went away.

Around the middle of the next semester, I became convinced a spot on my nose was cancerous, but a visit to the doctor assured me there was no medical problem. Both times I left the doctor feeling immensely relieved and a little foolish. Then I'd be fine for a while — until the next semester.

After a few such times of being obssessed with minor physical symptoms, I began to recognize the pattern and stopped to ask myself what was happening. Finally it occurred to me that these symptoms appeared just at the point when I was under the most pressure — when I knew I had to start studying in earnest and get to work on the term paper I dreaded writing — and a part of me wished I had a good excuse to just quit, drop out, and give it all up. If I were sick, no one could think the worse of me. What a relief not to have to work so hard, not to subject my family to all the problems that accompanied my return to school, not to feel guilty and selfish, to be able to stay dependent on my husband — in other words, not to have to suffer the death of old, familiar roles and grow into new, demanding, frightening ones.

When I realized what I was doing to myself, I was able to see that parts of my immature ego were, in effect, dying to make way for the fuller, more mature Self that was emerging in my conscious personality. That was why I was obsessed with dying. I hadn't learned yet how to tell the difference between psychological and physical death; in my pain and confusion, they felt the same to me. Recognizing this made it easier in subsequent semesters to deal with these little deaths of the old me, and by the time my course work was over these episodes no longer occurred.

I spent a long, busy, productive year writing my dissertation and defending it, and then, suddenly, I reached my goal — I received my doctorate and graduated! Did I feel marvelous? Only for a very short time. Then depression set in. The six months after graduation were as bad as the preceding three years had been, and death again became a frequent companion, sitting somewhere just behind my left shoulder. Every time I turned around, there it was.

I had learned from other graduate students to expect a letdown — it is a well-known phenomenon, sort of the postpartum depression of academia — but this was only part of the reason for my acute awareness of death. The greater reason was the death of my old self, for whom I had already been grieving for some time. My graduation — a rite of passage that marked the end of a very intense and rewarding phase of my life — had simply added another death to the one I was already experiencing. My work on the island was far from over.

This time, understanding the cause was not enough to make my fear of death go away; I had to find a new way to handle it. Instinctively I turned to writing poetry. I became addicted almost immediately. I was amazed at how fast the hours flew by when I worked on a poem, and I noticed that every time I finished one, I was filled with deep pride and an enormous sense of accomplishment. These pleasurable feelings, derived from creating something meaningful out of chaotic confusion, were almost like being under the influence of a powerful drug. But this was much better because there were no negative side effects: no hangover, no destructive behavior, no escaping from responsibilities, no neglecting of relationships, no remorse.

Over a three-month period I wrote about fifty poems that explored many of the feelings and changes I was experiencing. I didn't always understand everything I felt, but I struggled on, searching for words that would help me get a little closer to the truth of my experience. In looking back over this period of my life, I see that writing these poems was the best thing I could have done to heal myself and nurture the healthy growth going on within me.

First, this creative activity was nurturing because I was taking steps that were directly related to my pain and fear. If I'd decided to immerse myself in television or escapist books, I might have found some temporary relief, but I would have received no help for the source of my discomfort. In a way, psychological discomfort is like a disease — it most certainly is "dis-ease." Like an aspirin, television might have temporarily dulled the pain, but it would have done nothing to cure the cause of it. Writing about my difficulties, however, forced me to deal directly with them. Like a powerful X-ray, the process of creating poetry helped me to see what it was within me that was broken, undeveloped, or unhealthy. Only then could the correct remedy be found.

Second, I was doing something interesting and challenging.

I knew very little about writing poetry. My struggles with meter, rhyme, rhythm, figurative language, and the sounds and meanings of words were like going on a difficult quest. This laboring to master words, this shaping of them into a content and form that would most accurately represent my inner experience, was one of the most absorbing journeys I had ever undertaken. I was like a scientist seeking a star whose existence has long been suspected but never confirmed. I was seeking my own star — one that lay buried deep within me — and I was intoxicated with the heady excitement of the hunt.

Third, I was doing something creative. From out of the raw materials of my own confusion, discomfort, and need, small original works of art were emerging. It was like turning flour and water into bread, or a base metal into gold. And in the process of transforming my deepest longings into poems, I was transforming myself. Little by little, each poem I wrote brought me closer to the truth, closer to the new me that was being reborn. The words with which I wrestled had power — the power of Logos, the power to shed light on the dark places of my life.

It was not necessary that my creations be of publishable quality or deserve critical acclaim. The importance of what I was doing did not lay in the aesthetic quality of the finished product. In fact, when I look back at what I wrote, I'm embarrassed at the amateurish quality of some of the poems that once seemed so wonderful to me. The poems themselves are not important or even especially good, but the writing of them was everything.

The opening fairy tale in this book, "The Lily and the Rose," contains four lines from one of these poems, titled "Education":

> Then, finally, she finds the perfect flower,
> And when she puts it on, at last she knows
> That other lives cannot impart their power
> To one who seeks the lily but whose essence is the rose.

In this poem I tried to express how useless so much of my education had been, for it had in no way prepared me for the serious, painful search for myself that I was undergoing, or for my fearful encounters with the reality of death. As a result of these encounters, some of the poems were pretty grim and pessimistic. Others, however, like this simple little verse I wrote near the end of that period, are filled with hope:

The Voice of the Turtle

Like caterpillar dreaming of her wings,
My metamorphosis has just begun.
Like lark, who with the dawn prepares to sing,
The best I have to give is yet to come.

I know that this creative outpouring of my soul during this dark time was the very best thing I could have done for myself. Creative work has the power to heal even deep wounds. This is a mysterious phenomenon that cannot be completely understood but must simply be experienced. For me, the writing of poetry was the catalyst that began to heal my fear and pain, and it helped me make a successful transition into hope.

Since that time I've returned to the island on two other occasions when death's shadow tormented me. Although I didn't understand why then, I see in retrospect that in both cases some deep aspect of my being that I had outgrown and no longer needed was dying. In other words, my obsession with death was the result of an actual death of something very real in my unconscious.

The first time I returned to the island was during the death of a phase of my relationship with my daughter, who was preparing to go off to college. Interestingly enough, she experienced something similar. She had several dreams in which I died, and I had some disturbing dreams that heightened my awareness of my own death, too. In actuality, it was her childhood dependence on me and my need to keep her dependent that were dying — that, in fact, had to die in order for us to move more comfortably into this new phase of our lives. But to both of us, her birth into more independence felt like a death, and that's the way it came out in our dreams and everyday fears.

This time on the island I had no desire to write poetry. Instead, following some deep instinct, I gave myself a week in the month of April — a time of rebirth — to stay home and grieve. Without quite understanding what I was doing or why, I indulged myself in every possible way and simply let myself experience the emotions welling up within me. I stayed in my pajamas and robe all day, I ate when and what I felt like eating, I wept for no apparent reason, I screamed at the cat! By the fifth day, it was over. Not only was I ready to reenter my regular routine, but I felt refreshed and full of energy.

When the same thing happened again in my son's senior year of high school, I was only a little more prepared. Again, a precious phase of a relationship was dying. Again, both of us experienced this change as a fear of death.

During this same time I was also undergoing a powerful surge of self-doubt. I had publicly expressed some dissenting views to a group of male authority figures of a type that I had always tried hard to please. When a few of them let me know they disapproved of my opinions, all my childhood fear of censure from the male establishment came thundering back, and my tenuous new confidence in my right to be different was temporarily shattered.

Once again, I found solace in writing. It also helped to analyze my dreams. It was from them that I discovered the underlying sources of my fear. And this time I discovered something else. During the darkest week in which I was convinced that I would soon be dead, I also experienced the most intense and long-lasting periods of absolute bliss I had ever had. Everything and everybody became incredibly beautiful and dear to me, and I became softer, gentler, more grateful, more appreciative of every object, every person, every pleasurable sensation.

I've learned something from these experiences. First, each time they happen, they represent the death of something within me that has to die. If I allow myself to grieve and fully experience these deaths through creative work instead of denying them, once the necessary inner work has been accomplished, I emerge, as if from my dark and private island, renewed and energized.

Second, I've learned that fear of dying is not only natural and normal; it is, in fact, desirable. If we are to become free to accept our wholeness, we must learn to accept the wholeness of all of creation. This includes the dark side just as fully as the light side.

Getting to the bottom of our pain and honestly facing the reality of our own death is terrifying, but I believe that if we are to be reborn, it has to happen. Unless we are willing to confront the terrors of the dark, we will never be able to experience the ecstasy of the arrival of a new dawn. Facing the death of our bodies places everything in a different perspective. It makes us want to live fully in the time we have left, with every sense awake. It makes us slow down so we can relish every moment, each person, instead of rushing blindly about at the mercy of unconscious compulsions to assuage our shame and guilt or prepare for a tomorrow that may never come. It forces us to find a middle way between the search for our identity and our need to maintain meaningful relationships, to strive each day to find creative ways to reconcile these two opposing needs instead of living solely for one and neglecting the other.

The third thing I've learned is that the island experience is not something that happens only once in a lifetime. As long as I live on this earth, there will be times when I'll have to go back again to suffer, to examine myself, and to find my center. There is no way to escape the pain of decay and death, no way to live happily ever after without ever again having to change.

The island, that dark aspect of the feminine — the realm of mystery, instinct, and death — has much to teach us if we will take the time to learn. Facing death is the most terrible lesson, but it is also the best, for it is the lesson that forces us to expand beyond the limitations of our physical world and reach into the non-physical, subjective, unconscious realm. There we discover that there is so much more to us than our bodies or all the other things we can only know with our physical senses. There, through such things as dreams, visions, instincts, and intuitions, we get in touch with our souls, our guides to the spiritual realm. And the world of the spirit has really been our goal all along, for therein lies the source of the power that has created and nurtured the new birth growing within us.

18

The Wisdom of Dreams

MOVING CLOSER TO WHOLENESS by examining one's inner being on the island is essentially an act of creation, and in order to create anything, we must be willing to trust the source of our creativity. In psychological language, that source is not our rational, masculine, thinking mind, but the feminine unconscious. Carl Jung said, "The creative process has feminine quality, and the creative work arises from unconscious depths — we might say from the realm of the mothers."[1]

In our rational, masculine world it takes a great deal of effort to put aside our bias against the feminine, the nonrational, and the

---

[1] C.G. Jung, *Modern Man in Search of a Soul* (San Diego: Harcourt Brace Jovanovich, 1933), 170.

apparently illogical, and learn to trust the contents of the unconscious. Few of us are willing to "waste" our precious time on such an "impractical" endeavor. Usually the only people willing to rebel against the rut of mindless workaholism and stop to look within are artists or mystics — and aren't we just a little suspicious of these borderline malingerers?

What we do not realize is that exterior work must be balanced by interior work. Unless our outer work is an extension of our fuller authentic Selves, it can never satisfy, never be enough. And we can never hope to develop these Selves and thus find the satisfying, fulfilling work we were destined for if we are unwilling to go to the island within and do the hard inner work of bringing our dark, unconscious aspects into the light of consciousness.

Of all the ways I've discovered to get in touch with my unconscious, the most helpful has been to pay attention to my dreams. Because of some of my artistic and mystical tendencies, it was inevitable that I would begin to take dreams seriously during the third stage of my journey. When I realized that my dreams could help in my effort to get in touch with my fuller Self, I began to pay more attention to them. Some dreams recurred often enough that I had no trouble remembering them. Others were so interesting or had such a powerful impact on me that I wrote them down so I wouldn't forget them. Then a few years ago I decided to get serious, and I began to record every dream I could remember upon waking each morning. As of this writing, I've recorded over eleven hundred dreams, and I continue to marvel at their boundless wisdom and creativity.

To me, the unconscious is like a mysterious river that flows deep beneath the surface of my waking, conscious mind. The best way to get in touch with the refreshing water of this river is through a well, which is the clearest connection between my conscious and unconscious worlds. When I'm asleep and my ego is no longer in control, the bucket dips deep into the unconscious and brings back portions of the stream to relieve the thirst of my conscious mind. These drafts from my unconscious depths are dreams.

To me, dreams are real events that influence me every bit as much as the events in the outer world. But because I had been taught to think that only the outer world and outer events were "real," it was easy to consider the inner ones unimportant until I was in my island stage. Moreover, because these inner events can be so baffling to the conscious mind, it was very difficult to remember or understand them. Thus, I would forget my dreams, in which case their contributions to my conscious life went unnoticed. On the island, I began to write each one down in my dream journals so I could go back to my unconscious again and again, even when awake. By choosing to honor these inner events, I allowed my unconscious to honor me with helpful insights about myself.

Here is an example of the way my dreams have helped me to create a more authentic Self. While I was working on my doctorate and for some time afterward, I had three types of recurring dreams. In one, I was in a car that was moving forward dangerously fast. I had to put on the brakes, but for some reason it was always a struggle. Either I had to climb from the back seat into the front, which was enormously difficult; or I pushed the brake as far down as I could, but the seat was too far back and my foot wouldn't reach the floor and the car wouldn't stop.

In the second type of dream, I was scaling a steep mountain. When I neared the top, I'd suddenly find myself in a dangerous situation, dangling precariously over the edge or too high for comfort. In my fright I'd wonder what had compelled me to make this dangerous climb. Why was I here, when all I wanted was to be safe on the ground?

In the third type I would find myself going through a house I disliked and realize that I had, for some inexplicable reason, sold the house I loved to buy this one. This realization was always accompanied by a sense of profound sadness and loss.

While I didn't understand these dreams then, the meanings seem obvious now. The driving dreams represented my drivenness — my inability to put the brakes on my ambitious course. Unconsciously I wanted to stop my headlong dash down the road

I had chosen, but I was simply unable to. I was, indeed, driven.

The climbing dreams dramatically depicted my need to get to the top of my chosen profession, to go as high as I could go. These dreams were telling me I was aspiring to heights and a kind of success that were wrong for me, perhaps even dangerous to my psychological health.

The dreams of the unsuitable house were calling my attention to the fact that the place I was in, the place where I was living my psychic life at that time, was unsuitable to me at an unconscious level. I had neglected work I truly felt at home with (writing) to live in a house that was simply not right for me (teaching).

My goal at the time was to be a full-time college professor. I had been an adjunct instructor for several years, but I wanted a secure, tenure-earning position. Only then, I thought, could I be truly fulfilled. However, during that same period, I was beginning to realize that the traditional college classroom gave me little opportunity to teach the kinds of things that had become most meaningful to me: the personal, subjective things that help each of us solve the puzzle of our own lives. Moreover, teaching was so demanding that I had little time left to devote to writing, an activity I found increasingly enjoyable.

But oh, the status, the prestige, the self-satisfaction I would get from being a college professor! The admiration I would get from my family and friends. The gratification I would receive from being an object of respect to so many students who would look up to me with awe. The power! This was heady stuff, a hero myth form of success I had been taught to desire, and it was very difficult to give up. I preferred to believe that college teaching was my destiny. In my single-mindedness, I ignored the many signs and symptoms, including my dreams, that told me this job wasn't right for me. Tenaciously I continued to pursue my goal, and I continued to have the same dreams.

Finally, at a point when door after door had closed and my ambitions had been thwarted many times, I began to get the message. Maybe it was time to change directions. With mingled resignation and — somewhat to my surprise — relief, I quit teaching and began to write full-time.

Suddenly doors began to fly open. I was invited to present a paper at a conference. I met some publishers. I was offered some writing assignments. I had several articles, and then a book, published. Gradually I realized that writing was far more satisfying to me than college teaching. It was then that I remembered my deeply submerged, lifelong dream of being a writer, a dream I had abandoned at the age of ten because I believed that in order to ensure my future security I had better set my sights on a safer, more practical job like teaching or nursing.

After writing full-time for two years, I accepted a one-year position as a visiting assistant professor at a nearby university. I welcomed this opportunity to teach again because part of me still wondered if I had been right to give up teaching. Exactly two days after I completed this last college teaching job, I had a dream in which a woman companion and I were escaping from prison! Fifteen days later I dreamed I was walking through the most exquisite house I'd ever seen. In the dream it belonged to an actual woman friend who is a writer. The comfortable furniture, the color scheme, the beautiful polished oak staircase, the huge ballroom with two shiny black grand pianos placed back to back — everything about the house made it my dream house, a house I'd truly love to live in, and at the end of the dream I felt that it was to be my house. I woke up with a sense of awe that my unconscious could create such a beautiful place.

Since then I've never had my unsuitable house dreams again, and I have no more doubts about my true profession. And when I began to write this book, my unconscious confirmed the direction I had chosen, for I started dreaming about riding bicycles (which requires a great deal of balance) on quiet roads and climbing down from high, uncomfortable places and, with a sense of enormous relief, planting my bare feet firmly on warm, welcoming Mother Earth.

My dreams have taught me that gaining the admiration and

approval of others is a goal that can never satisfy my soul. My dreams have convinced me that authorities in the exterior world, no matter how wise or gifted, can never replace my own inner authority. I know that no matter how reliable or caring my friends and mentors were, none of them knew how to get within the heart of me and direct me to the work I was made for. I followed their advice, like a bee after honey, and still I wasn't happy, because nothing would ever taste as sweet as the nectar from my own inner blossoming. When I discovered my dreams, I found the only guide and authority who possessed the essence I had always sought: my Self.

Of all the tools I discovered on the island, learning to take my dreams seriously was the most meaningful and exciting. More than any other work I did there and continue to do — more than critical self-examination, reading, meditation, or prayer — analyzing my dreams has brought me closest to the spiritual realm and convinced me beyond doubt of the benevolent guidance of a divine source in my life. Dreams are the theater of the soul, our guide to the sacred. By learning to analyze the performances that are so lovingly produced for us every night, by heeding the messages from our unconscious and following their guidance, we are led to God.

19

Return to the Mother

THE DEATH PHASE OF OUR JOURNEY is a time when we feel lifeless and powerless. When we relinquish the comfort and safety of our castle walls, we abandon many of the resources that gave us the courage to go on. We are left with nothing to help us but a tiny, weak, and faltering voice — like the faint peeps from a baby chick still inside the egg — that is entirely unlike any voice we have ever heard before. This is the voice of the Self, the inner manifestation of God. If we are to get on with the experience of living, we need to allow the Self to be born into our conscious lives where we can avail ourselves of its new, creative resources.

The resources of our fuller Self come from beyond our conscious self. They come from the unconscious, from the spiritual realm, where they derive their creative power from a union of opposites. This union will not occur just because we consciously will it to. Logos may help us succeed in the outer world, but willpower and logical thought do not bring us to the kingdom of God. The spiritual union within ourselves happens only when we give up trying to control our own destinies and allow our true Logos and Eros — our masculine and feminine — aspects to unfold in our personalities. By allowing our full personalities to unfold, we are submitting to our divinely ordained destinies, to the nonrational mystery of a creative source beyond ourselves that we do not have to understand but must only give in to.

In *The Kingdom Within*, John Sanford states that by developing our personalities we experience the kingdom of God. In explaining the meaning of two of Jesus' parables about the kingdom of God, he writes:

> The kingdom is both that which we find within ourselves as an inner treasure and also that which is searching to find us, who when found become something of supreme value in the eyes of God . . . . When we find and realize the kingdom in ourselves, we experience a growing wholeness, an increasing sense of the meaning of our individual personality, a realization of new and creative energies, and an expanding consciousness . . . . The kingdom involves the realization of our personalities according to the inner plan established within us by God . . . [1]

This means that the painful process of self-confrontation that leads to inner understanding and wholeness is our spiritual task and our ultimate destiny as ordained by God.

On this earth we have been given a model of creativity and unity that requires a joining of the masculine and the feminine. Only in this way can new life be created. If we are created in the

---

[1] John A. Sanford, *The Kingdom Within: The Inner Meaning of Jesus' Sayings* (San Francisco: Harper & Row, 1987), 27, 28.

image of God, then God, too, must be composed of both the masculine and the feminine principles. Otherwise, God could not possibly have created anything.

Yet, to most of us, God is "Our Father who art in heaven," a holy force outside of ourselves. It occurs to few of us that God might also be "Our Mother who art within us." This interpretation, however, explains the paradox of a God who is not only an outer seeker but also an inner treasure. It also explains the natural tendency humans have to assign seeking, questing, penetrating, goal-oriented behaviors to the masculine, while attributing resting, nurturing, receiving, waiting-to-be-awakened behaviors to the feminine. While these characteristics do not necessarily correspond to actual behaviors exclusive to one sex or the other, they do provide us with a way of organizing the two opposing natures we recognize in the world and in ourselves. There is not only a God-like voice outside of ourselves that calls us, but also a Goddess-like voice within us that responds.

On the island we uncover our biases against the parts of ourselves we rejected in our youth. When we see our bias against the feminine principle of Eros and allow it to emerge in our personalities, we rediscover the abandoned and scorned feminine aspect of God and avail ourselves of Her power.

If we are to approach wholeness, we must accept the feminine aspect of God. We do not have to reject or abandon the Father, for the masculine aspect of God is also part of the deity, but we *must* return to the Mother.

A return to the Mother involves many things. One is developing connections to the unconscious Self so that we allow it to influence our conscious, daily lives in creative ways that are exactly right for us. Another is coming to grips with our mortality — in other words, facing and accepting death. Still another is allowing the feminine principle of Eros to be born within ourselves, which means being willing to be deeply, emotionally related to life, to our bodies, to our instincts, and to other people. Another is accepting ourselves as we are and becoming real, honest, authentic individuals.

We can better understand the Great Mother, or the feminine aspect of God, if we look at the human experience of being a mother. Of all the roles available to women today, none is so sublime or so mundane as that of mother. Nothing makes one feel more powerful or more helpless. Nothing makes the divine so imminent or the earth so intimate, nothing makes immortality seem so tangible or death so inevitable, nothing brings so much joy or so much grief, as motherhood.

Motherhood — the experience that forges bonds of indissoluble relatedness to one's beautiful, vulnerable, very own child — forces one to experience and reconcile the ultimate opposites: fertility, or life, and sterility, or death. It is this perpetual containment within oneself of the tension of the opposites that supplies the energy to release feminine power. In a human mother this power takes the form of such extreme courage and devotion that she is able to sacrifice everything — her own comfort, her own needs, her own happiness, even her own life — in order to nurture the growth and preserve the life of another.

The power of the Mother is the opposite of traditional masculine power in every way: It is receptive instead of aggressive; nourishing and preserving instead of dividing and diminishing; bent on forgiveness instead of revenge; focused on making peace with one's inner dragons instead of conquering them in the outside world; warmly passionate instead of coldly logical; connected and related instead of superior and remote; and strong and courageous in the inner world of emotions, not just the outer world. Finally, this power is characterized by a deep, instinctual spirituality, as opposed to one that is lofty, pure, and intellectual.

Motherhood is the ultimate teacher of the Eros lessons of relatedness and connection. And we must all, male and female, learn these lessons of the Great Mother if we are to regain the abundance of our wholeness; experience the rare gift of the blissful, brimming, bursting fullness of our personalities; and become aware at last of the sufficient beauty of being alive.

Many women begin to learn these lessons when they are pregnant. The woman who experiences a child growing within her body is forced to submit passively to forces of nature far stronger than herself. This forced submission teaches her the lesson of humility. At the same time it empowers her with an inner confidence and authority that men can only wonder at. In the mother's recognition that there is something more powerful than her own ego and that she is defenseless before this power, she is initiated into the spiritual realm.

Of course, men and women who are not mothers also seek and find admittance to this realm, but they are not usually forced to undergo initiations that require them to sacrifice their egos for the sake of connectedness. Thus, masculine spirituality often remains intellectualized, while feminine spirituality has a different quality — a quality of quiet confidence and certainty. Like a brooding hen who sits serenely on her eggs, the mother knows, without need of words, that she is being used to fulfill a purpose that is greater and higher than any that mere humans can devise.

To men who are not in touch with their feminine sides, the life-giving creative force is a beautiful idea. They see this idea embodied in women, and they therefore feel compelled to control women, just as they wish to control life itself. To women it is not an idea — it is a concrete reality. For women embody life. This is true of all women, whether or not they ever become biological mothers.

I was intimately aware of the creative force even as a very young child. I just lost touch with it for a while. The story of my own journey back to the Mother began when I was seven. That year my father bought us a house in Tampa. Soon afterward, his mother came for a visit. Grandma Benedict was a strong woman of unusual intellect. She was also deeply religious. One day when my parents were at work and my brother was outside playing war with his friends, she decided to tell me about God.

She began with an observation about my brother's game. "I don't approve of those boys playing war," she said sternly. "War is not a game. War is cruel and evil. People get killed in wars.

That's not what God wants for us." Then she went on to tell me about a God of love and peace. When she was finished, she asked if I wanted to dedicate my life to God. I said yes, so together we knelt beside my bed and she told me what to say.

This woman was not the soft, cozy grandmother of children's stories — the kind who makes delicious cookies and tells wonderful stories, as my maternal grandmother did. Grandma Benedict was a tough, serious-minded perfectionist. Nevertheless, she gave me a wondrous gift that day: She gave me the gift of Logos — words that I could use to help me understand and express the divine mystery that I had already felt deep in my bones. These words were necessary. Until this point I had only had a diffused awareness, a deep Eros sense (perhaps erotic is a better word to explain the exuberant attitude I had about life then) of being connected to something awesome and magnificent, with unlimited beauty and power. And, thanks to my grandmother, I at last had a name for this awareness: God.

My grandmother also demonstrated her own Eros nature. She wanted to tell me about God because she felt connected to me through her son, my father. Without realizing it, she was honoring her own, highly repressed Eros nature, even though she only knew how to do it with masculine/Logos words. Her sense of connection to me came out of her feminine experience of being a mother. Growing up in the place and time she did, Grandma Benedict could not express an awareness of the Eros aspect of God, but in accordance with her feminine nature, she honored it anyway. It was her powerful love for me and her deep sense of connectedness to the Divine Being that compelled her to kneel beside me on the floor and show me how to commit myself to something greater than myself.

After praying with her, I became consciously aware of my connection with a sacred mystery that seemed to be present in everything. It was so wonderfully real to me that I would look in bewilderment at the adults whose behavior often demonstrated that they did not seem to know the secret I knew. I couldn't figure out how that could be, because I naturally assumed that adults knew everything. But when I would hear my minister try to convince people about the existence of God and exhort them to faith, I realized that they, and perhaps even he, didn't really share in the secret. If they knew what I knew, they wouldn't have to be reminded all the time. They could just enjoy! But they didn't seem to understand this, and I never heard anyone speak of the special kind of awareness I had. So I kept my secret to myself and privately celebrated my blissful existence as a blessed child of God in a divinely created world.

But a few years later, shortly after my baptism — a lovely but perfunctory ceremony that seemed to have been invented to convince people of something I already knew — I began to lose my quiet certainty about my connection to the deity. My parents divorced, and then my father died. That's when much of my vitality and boundless sense of personal power died, too. I needed safety in the frightening physical world that had such cruel power to wound, so I began to neglect many of my natural feminine resources.

From that time on, I began to look for spiritual assurances from the masculine world. Reason, belief in doctrines, good deeds, and striving for moral goodness and spiritual purity did, indeed, tide me over nicely for quite some time. But once in a while, something would happen to remind me that there was more to God than could be logically understood by the mind.

For example, when I was in my early thirties an event occurred that made no logical sense at all. My husband and I were at a church weekend retreat. On Saturday evening after the group meeting, a friend came up to us and asked if we would go outside and speak to her daughter, a college student who was in deep distress. I had absolutely no idea how we could help, but we agreed to go.

We found the daughter sitting outside in the dusk on a bench under an old oak tree. Her boyfriend had his arm around her to comfort her as she sat there weeping. I sat on the other side of her, feeling totally inadequate, wishing I were a wiser person. Then I did the only thing I knew to do. I put my hands on her shoulders and began to pray. I think my husband did, too.

I don't remember if we prayed silently or aloud, but as I touched her I began to be filled with a tremendous feeling of despair. And I, a person who never cried in public, who didn't even cry when my father died, began to cry. I wept silently at first, but my crying soon turned into deep, wrenching sobs. Oddly enough, the harder I cried, the less she cried, until at last she had stopped completely and I was crying alone.

A part of me stood off observing myself with wonder. How could I be doing such a thing? Where was my sense of pride? What must these people think of me? Yet something deep inside felt so right that I allowed myself to give in to this instinctive, unexplainable behavior.

When I had finally finished crying, I hugged the young woman in embarrassment and said I hoped she would feel better soon. She said thank you, and I escaped through the blessed darkness to my cabin. For the remainder of the weekend I avoided her and her boyfriend, for I was humiliated by my emotional public display. But I knew that *something* had happened. Somehow I had felt deeply connected to her and had given in to something within myself that had enabled me to absorb her pain and grief and momentarily share her burden. And the sense of awe I felt over this experience told me that this something had the touch of the divine.

Through the years I saw other examples of the feminine side of God, but in my commitment to the safe and explainable masculine God of the church, I remained consciously unaware of Her. But then I was compelled to challenge the Father and follow the Golden Bear to the island. My time had come at last to rediscover my feminine essence and recover the power of the Mother.

As we accommodate ourselves to the masculine world, most of us forget the extraordinary feminine power that we sensed in ourselves or our mothers when we were very young. The more we deny feminine life-giving power, the more we try to extinguish the feminine aspect of the divine light and cling only to the masculine aspect, the more one-sided we become. Then we become fully immersed in a dark prison where the Father's light — a light composed of logic and reason and purity and perfection, a light which once seemed like the only answer — is no longer sufficient to show us the way for the rest of our lives. Bu putting out the Mother's light — the light of instinctual, authentic feeling, connection, and the understanding heart — we have smothered our own vital essence until all we can think of is the reality of life's opposite: death.

In order to begin to remember about life, we must first allow the deity to manifest its dark side. Most of us will do anything to avoid this. We will focus only on the outer hero journey and become so involved with our accomplishments that our terrified egos will not have to confront death. Unfortunately, as long as death stays submerged in our unconscious, we will not be able to fully enjoy life, and we will have no idea why.

But when we are forced to face the death of an important relationship or a beloved aspect of ourselves or a person we love, then, at last, we can begin to make our inner journeys to the island. This is because we have finally experienced firsthand the fundamental connectedness to another human being that is indigenous to the Mother. Only by facing the loss of this physical connection are we able to move our focus from the physical realm to the spiritual one to seek the resources we need to live the remainder of our lives.

Once we have faced death and made a choice for life, we begin to remember the feminine side of God. Gradually She will manifest Herself in a growing awareness of the splendor of the life-giving force as it exists in all of creation. It is this awareness — a quiet certainty that never goes away, and an almost constant sense of awe as we stand before Her boundless capacity to create and nourish and protect — that gives new meaning to life. This is what enables us to feel fully alive and to enjoy our work and relationships and everything life has to offer with enthusiasm, creativity, and vitality. Our connection to this power also helps us endure the worst without losing faith, balance, or the ability to love strongly and feel deeply.

We cannot acquire these powerful resources of the Great Mother through wordy exhortations to faith, pure thoughts, or intellectual exercises. The human mind may be the way to get in touch with the masculine aspect of God, but the Mother is approached through the body and the heart. The Mother's power becomes available to us only through physical, deeply emotional experiences that force us to make difficult choices to honor the feminine principle of Eros or relatedness. As we develop reverence for the feminine and build an inner bridge to unite her with the masculine, new life is created, just as new life is created when the male sperm and the female egg are united. This is when we begin to hear the voice of the Self at last.

When this happens, our island work is still not finished, for then we must learn to tell the difference between the voice of our immature old ego self and the wonderful new Self that is being born. But eventually, sharp listening and probing questions will yield their reward: a wondrous, surging emergence out of confusion and darkness.

As I endured my island experience, my pain and suffering and fear of death gradually receded, and they were replaced by a mighty upsurge of power — a creative, life-giving, joyful potency that would enable me to build a bridge back into the outer world where I could at last function as the healthy mature adult I was meant to be. I felt I was being reborn and, in a way, I was.

Witnessing my own rebirth was an awesome experience. As painful as it was, I have never been sorry for having endured it. I emerged from the darkness of the inner journey, strengthened and ready to introduce the Self I had discovered there to the conscious light of the outer world. When my eyes, fast-blinking, adjusted to the brilliant light and I dared to look around, I found that I was standing, amidst broken eggshells, on holy ground.

PART FOUR
A Time of Rebirth

20

The Wedding

FOR THOSE MAKING THE JOURNEY, the island is like a chrysalis that has sheltered a tender mutation. For the princess who has lived for relationship but has discovered it is not enough, the task on the island has been to develop her individuality, and it is her metamorphosis into a creature who can reconcile the two that builds the bridge to wholeness. For the hero who has successfully pursued his calling in the outer world, his need for authentic relationship has brought him to the island and determined the nature of his work there. In either case, when we finally honor the opposing claims of individuation and relationship, when we learn how to maintain a delicate balance between them both, we begin to build a bridge back to the outer world where meaningful work and meaningful relationships await. Then we are reborn into a newer, fuller person.

Building this inner bridge is a slow and gradual process. The bridge does not suddenly appear out of the blue; it is built step by step, in the same way that a bridge is built in the physical world, through diligent inner work and persistent, daily attention to the status of our inner and outer conditions. Because the progress is so slow and each step forward so subtle, many years may pass before we consciously realize we have made an important transition.

In my case, I gradually became aware of small signs of change. For example, I found increasing pleasure in many things I had simply taken for granted before: a sunset, a flower, my home, my body, a hug or a smile from my husband or children. I also noticed changes in my relationships with others: I was really listening to what they said, seeing their points of view, and responding to each situation in honest, creative ways instead of out of blind habit. I was more patient with myself and others, more tolerant of flaws, quicker to forgive, more peaceful. And I was much more confident about my ideas and opinions, more willing to express them and less fearful of the judgments of others. As these and other signs began to occur more often, and as my feelings of fear, self-doubt, shame, and guilt dwindled and appeared less frequently, I realized that my inner work was paying off.

Then, about two years ago, my unconscious Self confirmed my rebirth. I dreamed that I was invited to attend the wedding of a woman named Jeanie:

> *I'm at a big house where the wedding will be held. I'm upstairs looking out a window. There's a large book outside on the ledge. It's full of pictures. I want this book very badly, but it's too near the ledge and I'm suddenly aware of how high I am. I'm afraid I'll fall if I step out to get it. I step back inside the window and slam it shut. The movement jars the book and it falls to the ground. I have to go downstairs all the way to the ground to get the book. As I reach the bottom and prepare to walk outside, some people I don't know come in and bring the book to me.*

I go back inside to watch the wedding. The bride comes over to me and says, "You look so wonderful. Do you know you look more and more like [a long, Russian-sounding name I can't remember]*?" She looks at me earnestly and I feel greatly complimented. Then I ask if there's a book I can read about this woman I'm beginning to look like and she says there is.*

The wedding is taking place. I'm sitting behind rows of people who are standing in front of me. I can't actually see the bride and groom, but I catch occasional glimpses of dancers, bright lights, and beautiful flashing colors way up front where the couple is getting married.

I had this powerful dream at the beginning of my last year of teaching. I didn't know it was to be my last year, because I still thought I might want to continue to teach. But something very different from my conscious orientation was taking place in my unconscious.

I was at the end of the death phase of my journey and was entering a far more rewarding phase — the phase when the bridge between my intuitive feminine qualities and my intellectual masculine qualities was strong enough to enable me to cross back and forth at will. And I was writing at last. I was finishing a book about television literacy (a "picture" book?). My dream told me that when that book was finished, there would be another book in my future, a book about my newly transformed self. The new book the bride told me about would be my creation, my child — *this book.*

If I had stayed in the ivory tower of education, that lofty, uncomfortable, Logos-dominated realm of the intellect, I would have been in danger of losing my "picture" book and this one, too. But somehow my unconscious knew I had reached the point where I needed so badly to write that I would come all the way down to Mother Earth to obtain my book. Only if I stepped down from the world of the university could certain elements within my unconscious personality aid me in retrieving something that I needed; something that my Self wanted so much to give to me.

The bride — my beautiful, inner, virginal feminine aspect — was deeply interested in me and proud of the changes occurring within me. Even though I wasn't consciously aware of this, she was ready for the wedding with my masculine aspect, a man I didn't actually see in that dream but whom I would get to know in other dreams when he would appear as a writer, a pilot, a helpful stranger, a cowboy, a priest, or my Beloved.

And then, in my dream, the wedding took place and it was so dazzling I wasn't allowed to behold it. But the wedding happened and I changed irrevocably, even though at first I had no conscious idea of what this dream meant. And gradually, and oh so gently, my dreams began to make their subtle suggestions and this book came to be written. All along, "something" was at work in my unconscious world guiding me toward a new, fulfilling destiny.

The archetype of the wedding, the symbolic union between the masculine and the feminine, is deeply ingrained within the human psyche. The implications of the wedding for the spiritual welfare of humans are so profound that within many religions it has attained the status of a sacrament. Like all sacraments, it pertains to both an inner and an outer reality. In our outwardly oriented society, we tend to stress only the outer reality and to ignore the inner one. But the underlying psychological meaning of the wedding is just as important to our inner well-being as the physical union is to our outer lives.

Anima is a feminine word meaning the inner breath of life or vital principle, i.e., the soul, spirit, or mind; *animus* is the masculine version of the same thing. The psychologist Carl Jung used *anima* to refer to a man's inner feminine aspects and *animus* when discussing a woman's inner masculine self. When a woman gets in touch with all the feminine aspects of her mind, soul, and spirit, yet at the same time develops a relationship with her animus and allows him to become a conscious part of her personality, a sacred inner marriage takes place. The same thing happens when a man develops his masculinity, yet also accepts the presence and powerful influence of his anima.

Only when this sacred inner union takes place, only when we accept ourselves and develop an intimate relationship with our opposite in the inner world, is the birth of the divine child made possible. In religion, dreams, folk literature, and mythology, the divine child is a symbol for humankind's ultimate achievement: the birth of creative, liberating, redeeming new life.

How sad it is that because of long-standing prejudices against the feminine, so much of humankind has been deprived of the opportunity to experience this inner rebirth. Although long ago the feminine was deeply revered, over the last five millennia most people have believed the feminine way to be inferior to the masculine. We are finally beginning to understand that there is nothing inherently superior or inferior about either sex, and that there is as much power within the feminine principle as there is within the masculine. We can see that an infinitely greater, vastly more creative power is released when mutual respect builds a bridge that connects men and women to each other in the outer world just as it connects the masculine and feminine aspects within each individual.

Without the feminine, life is incomplete. When we accept the feminine, we know the sensuous sweetness of directly experiencing life, with its joy and sorrow, without having to define or trick or defeat or control it. We discover a liberating release when we allow ourselves to submit to feelings and open ourselves up to give and receive tenderness and warmth. We experience a resurgence of vitality when we risk being vulnerable, passionate, or different.

Life is equally incomplete without the masculine. Women who seek wholeness must learn to trust their inner animus for the masculine qualities they need. By befriending the inner masculine and allowing it to exist peacefully beside the inner feminine, women can bridge the gap that has historically separated us from our hope for completeness.

Moreover, when we avail ourselves of our own masculine qualities, we free the men in our lives from the burden of always having to direct us, approve of us, solve our problems, keep us safe, and make us happy. Then, instead of expecting perfection from our partners and being angry when they disappoint us, we are able to establish intimate, meaningful relationships with them. We can accept and love them for what they truly are: real, flawed human beings who, just like us, are struggling along on difficult journeys of their own.

As my inner work has brought me closer to my Self, it has enhanced every aspect of my life, including my relationship with my husband. Both of us have changed in many ways. Getting in touch with my feelings has freed us both from having to guess and pretend and tiptoe around each other. Once I realized that I was as important as he was, and had as much right to have my needs met as he had, I started being honest with him about my feelings, and I began to please myself as much as I had always pleased him. It has not been easy for either of us; change is never easy. But because we are both committed to our relationship, and because we have been willing to persevere despite the inevitable difficulties that neither of us was prepared for, our hard work has paid off, so much so that we have a lovely relationship in which we are both usually able to voice our needs honestly and negotiate conflicts.

And now that we understand and accept each other much better, it is amazing how much we enjoy each other's company. Sometimes my tears flow out of sheer thankfulness for the way he has enriched my life. Much of the time when I'm with him, I feel a deep sense of peace. I guess it shows. When we went to Europe for our twenty-fifth anniversary, a younger couple on their honeymoon asked us if we were newlyweds. They couldn't get over how much in love we were.

There is no doubt in my mind that this man and I were destined for each other. We are very different, and our differences complement, nurture, and prod each other in many positive ways. For me, being married to him is proof that I am loved by something much bigger than myself. For me, he is a bridge to the sacred realm.

Truly intimate, authentic relationships are possible when we experience rebirth as a result of the union of the masculine and feminine principles. This inner union is the deepest meaning behind the sacred ritual of the wedding. The symbolic inner marriage is available to seekers everywhere. It is not an easy way, but it is worth taking, for it is the way that the creative principle — the divine child — is born within us.

21

The Feminine Quest

THE WAY TO THE INNER WEDDING, or the bridge, is through
the persistent inward journey to the island, a symbol that stands
in the same relationship to the feminine heroine as the monster or
enemy does to the masculine hero. Island work is never completed, but is carried on throughout the duration of our lives.
However, once the bridge is built, our visits to the island are never
as cataclysmic as that first time, when it was a dreaded last resort
to alleviate frightful suffering. In fact, the more often we visit the
island and become accustomed to its work, the closer we stay to
the center of the bridge where we are equally comfortable communicating with outer or inner companions.

The island is the place where we come to accept our inner
opposites and begin to be reborn into mature individuals who can

see and embrace our own splendor. The road there is filled with detours and hardships. When called to the island, we must be careful not to settle for incomplete substitutes along the way. The knight who ends his quest for individuation prematurely out of apathy or fear, the princess who settles for a superficial relationship with the prince because she does not want to annoy him or risk ruining her carefully prepared façade of perfection — these people never break through their walls, never visit the island, never develop their opposite potential, never experience rebirth. And they are never able to build the bridge between their inner and outer selves.

Since doing my initial island work, I've had several dreams about bridges, but this is the one that began to teach me the basic difference between the masculine and feminine journeys to wholeness.

> *A man and I are on opposite sides of a bridge with a road running between us. We're both reclining on benches that line the sides of the bridge. I'm reclining to the left; he's reclining to the right. We're friends, and we're talking to each other across the bridge.*

Until I understood this dream, I couldn't figure out why the traditional hero myth simply is not adequate to explain a woman's quest. Certainly men and women have equal abilities, equal intelligence. Both sexes are capable of achieving their destinies in the outer world as well as allowing their personalities to unfold through inner work.

Why then does the masculine hero only get the hand of the princess (an inner relationship with his anima) *after* he accomplishes outer work? Why was my journey so different? Why was I never able to find satisfaction in my accomplishments in the outer world? Why did I have to do my inner work and learn to trust my femininity and develop relationships with my animus and other inner characters *before* I could find my reward in my outer life?

I struggled with these questions for many months. But the dream gave me an important clue. In the dream, my male friend was leaning to my right, which, in the symbolic language of dreams, means the outer world. I, however, was inclined toward my left, or the inner world. We were both on the same bridge, and we were able to communicate with each other across the road. But we were on opposite sides and we were oriented in opposite directions.

As someone whose essence was masculine, my friend was oriented to the outer world; however, as a person whose essence was feminine, I was oriented to the inner world. His primary task was outer work, and he needed to develop and test his personal skills in the outer realm before he would be able to generate a connection with the inner world. But for me the opposite was true: Inner work was the primary task before I could acquire a meaningful connection with the outer world.

Perhaps this explains why so many men seem to make their most noticeable contributions to the outer world in their early years and then retire to lives of quiet contemplation in later age. Alexander the Great, Napoleon, and William the Conqueror are only a few examples of the masculine need to prove oneself in the outer world during the youthful years. All these men changed the course of history before their fifties. Perhaps their later, less visibly active years, were spent in inner work, thus completing the cycle to wholeness.

But the feminine quest for wholeness takes a different route. For most women, the journey does not begin in the outer world. A woman may be extremely effective at her work — certainly she can compete and produce as well as men — but as long as she continues to follow the masculine model of the hero myth without doing her inner work, she is doomed to frustration. This may explain why so much depression occurs in middle-aged women who have worked long and hard at their jobs, expecting to find fulfillment. They may have become extremely successful by the standards of the masculine world, yet they are exhausted, depressed, miserable, and sometimes even ill, and they have no idea why.

One reason for their pain may be that they have forfeited their feminine journeys in order to conform to the masculine model of frenzied dragon-slaying, to become individuated by proving themselves in the outer world. A woman can find status in the outer world, but if she seeks wholeness, she must go inward to the island to make peace with her dragons before she can become individuated. Once she gets in touch with her unconscious world and learns how to be true to her Self, she discovers how to express her unique talents and skills in meaningful ways in the outer world, while at the same time maintaining meaningful relationships.

The problem with our thinking about the way to achieve wholeness is that we have been operating from within a patriarchal world-view for so long. We have emphasized the outer, physical world of masculine accomplishments and have ignored the inner, feminine world of introspection. In this one-sided view, men and women are expected to be fulfilled if they function successfully in the outer world. The better they perform their duties — in other words, the more money they are able to make, or the cleaner they are able to keep their castles, or the better the schools they are able to send their children to — the happier they are supposed to be. If they are unable to find happiness this way, then it is assumed there is something wrong with them: They must be whiners or weaklings or wimps. Few ever stop to consider that there might be something wrong with such a one-sided interpretation of the meaning of life.

Wholeness cannot be attained by ignoring our inner Selves. Denying the influence of the unconscious does not make our inner Self go away. It only makes us more confused and unhappy and sick and bitter. In order to move into wholeness, we must balance outer, masculine accomplishments with the interior journey to the feminine island.

The differences between one-sided patriarchal interpretations and the fuller, authentic masculine and feminine journeys can be illustrated with a mandala (see next two pages). Imagine a

Journey of the Patriarchal Hero

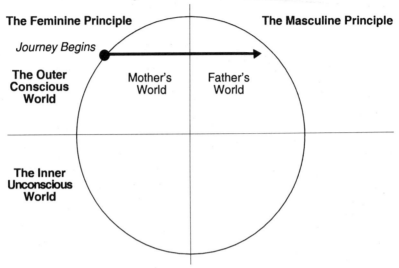

The Authentic Hero Journey

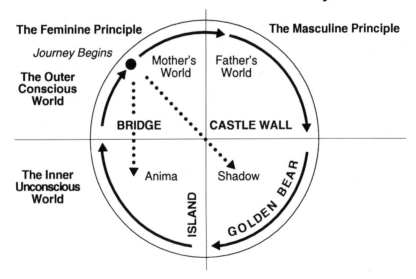

Journey of the Patriarchal Princess

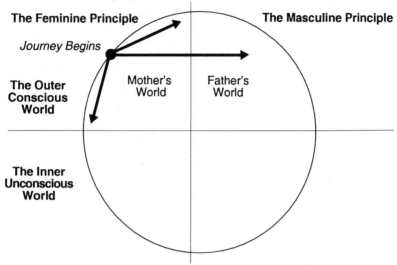

The Authentic Feminine Quest

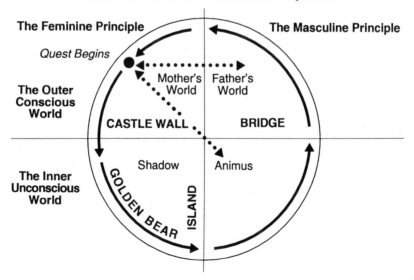

circle that represents wholeness. Divide the circle into four quarters. The upper half of the circle represents the outer, conscious world where heroic works are displayed for all to see; the lower half represents the inner, unconscious world, or the realm of the island where an invisible, feminine kind of heroism takes place. The right half of the circle represents the masculine principle; the left half the feminine principle.

Patriarchy's interpretation of the hero myth takes place only in the exterior, conscious world. This linear journey is depicted in the mandala at the top of the page. The patriarchal hero is expected to leave the security of his Mother's world, where he has been nourished, loved, and protected, and move as quickly as possible into the Father's world. Some men refuse to be heroes and cling to the Mother's world for their entire lives by trading in their mothers for wives who will fulfill the same role. But the patriarchal hero moves on into the Father's world where he slays dragons and accomplishes daring deeds. Once a man becomes independent of his mother and proves himself in the Father's world, he is considered to be a hero and expected to be content with his work and his reward: his wife.

In its focus on the exterior world, patriarchy has failed to develop the underlying meaning of the hero's feminine reward; but the authentic hero knows something is missing. He senses his need to develop an intimate relationship with the feminine. This is where the journey to wholeness begins: when he breaks away from conformity to patriarchal standards and acknowledges the presence and influence of the interior world.

The journey of the authentic hero is depicted at the bottom of the page. It is a circular rather than linear journey that moves to the right in a clockwise direction. It begins in the same place where the patriarchal hero started his journey — in the Mother's world. Like the patriarchal hero, the authentic hero must also leave his mother and develop his own skills so he can become an independent individual in the Father's world. But here the similarities end: The authentic hero is the one who hears the call of the

Golden Bear and acknowledges its influence. This call lures him into the wilderness of the unconscious. He may first become aware of the call while he is still in the Mother's world, and it continues to haunt him while he is busy conforming to the patriarchal standards of the Father's world. While honing his skills and developing his individuality, the authentic hero makes occasional forays into the dangerous wilderness and becomes increasingly aware of its powerful influence on his life.

Influence from the unconscious world is depicted in the mandala of The Authentic Hero Journey by dotted lines. These temporary visits into the unconscious can take many forms: questioning traditional goals, self-examination, therapy, renewed interest in religion, reading, poetry-writing, occasional dream work, creative hobbies, and so on. These forays are essential to the hero's development because the more he can acknowledge the influence of his unconscious, the more courage he acquires to make the eventual break through the castle wall. This break occurs when dragon-slaying becomes so meaningless that he has no other choice but to search for the true reward for which he yearns: completion, which means an intimate relationship with the feminine.

In order to establish intimacy with the feminine and become complete, the authentic hero must make a conscious commitment to conduct his inner work. He needs to break through the castle walls that have confined his focus to the outer world, persist in following the Golden Bear through the dark wilderness, and journey to the island. I suspect that for most heroes, especially very successful ones, serious inner work seems even more dangerous and threatening than dragon- slaying.

On the island he meets all the feared, unknown aspects of his masculinity. This is his dark side, or shadow. He has probably already learned some things about his shadow from interactions with his parents and his peers, but it is time to make a concerted effort to understand and accept this dark side. Only after he makes peace with those aspects of his personality that he has spent his life rejecting and denying is he able to cross the barrier to establish a relationship with his mysterious unconscious feminine potential, his anima.

Until he comes to the island, a man's feminine side might appear to be a dreaded enemy. Because he has not allowed her to become a conscious part of his personality, she has probably influenced his personality and relationships with others, especially women, in negative ways. But once a man begins to accept his shadow side, he is free to establish a relationship with his inner feminine and she becomes a trusted friend.

If he persists in his inner work, the inner marriage takes place. This produces an internal explosion that fills him with renewed awe at the beauty of life and causes a powerful resurgence of creativity and vitality that will remain with him for the rest of his life. Union with his inner feminine also enables him to develop a conscious, intimate, satisfying relationship with the feminine in the exterior world. Then the journey is complete and the true meaning of the hero myth has been fully developed: The hero has built a bridge back to the feminine and is becoming a whole person.

Like the patriarchal hero, the patriarchal princess begins her journey in the Mother's world. As long as she continues to conform, she will vacillate between two alternatives. She can remain in the castle where she lives solely for relationships for her entire life; if she gets married she simply trades the castle of her parents for the castle of her husband. Or she can move into the Father's world of work and live the masculine hero myth. Or she can try to do both at the same time. Regardless of what she chooses, the patriarchal princess rejects the call of the Golden Bear, assuming that outer relationships or outer work will bring happiness and fulfillment.

A woman like this may develop some of her masculine potential in the exterior world, but this is not the same thing as acquiring a conscious, loving relationship with her animus, her masculine side; the inner marriage only occurs with serious inner work. Only when she gets in touch with her unconscious, and learns to accept and understand it, will her true feminine energy and creativity be released. Without these necessary resources, the Mother's world of relationships and the Father's world of work only become increasingly frustrating.

As the mandala of The Authentic Feminine Quest shows, when a woman finally develops the strength to leave the castle and begin her quest for wholeness, she moves in the opposite direction from that of the masculine hero. Her quest takes her to the left, or counter-clockwise. Unlike men, women do not need to separate themselves from the feminine in order to become individuated; but they do need to leave the outer world of conformity where they have tried to remain safe.

I think it is possible for a woman to bypass forays into the Father's world altogether and go straight from the Mother's world (either her childhood castle or her husband's castle where she, herself, is a mother) to the island, where she first establishes a relationship with her repressed feminine and then unites with her inner masculine. Emily Dickinson, for example, was able to become individuated and experience the inner marriage with her creative animus without ever competing or climbing the ladder in the outer Father's world. Most women of today, however, begin their journeys into the unconscious only after they have developed some of their masculine potential through forays into the Father's world, perhaps by going back to school or getting a job. This is necessary for most women because it gives them the strength and courage they failed to develop as long as they conformed to patriarchal standards and remained dependent on men for these qualities.

Development of her masculine potential is shown by the dotted lines on the mandala of The Authentic Feminine Quest. As long as a woman vacillates between individuation and relationships, this movement goes back and forth in a linear way. She develops some of her masculine potential, but she is not in full, conscious control of it; rather, it drives her and pushes her into greater and greater deeds. She may appear to be a successful wife or successful executive, but she has not yet come to recognize her individuality or develop a deep reverence for her full, true, complete Self, in all its feminine and masculine aspects.

To find out who she really is, a woman needs to go deeper into the feminine, to proceed into the inner world of the island — the lower half of the mandala. There she first encounters her shadow, the repressed parts of her personality and potential. As she makes peace with her dark feminine aspects, she becomes strong enough to cross the barrier into the realm of her unknown masculine potential. There, at last, she begins to develop a conscious relationship with her animus.

After a woman faces her unknown and rejected masculine and feminine aspects, and connects them by means of an inner marriage or bridge, the feminine quest then proceeds up into the conscious world. After the woman has become individuated and established a relationship between her inner masculine and feminine, she can begin to express her herself in uniquely creative ways in the outer world where meaningful work and intimate relationships await.

But this is not the end of the journey for a woman. She completes the circle and moves into wholeness by moving back to the world of the Mother, where she at last becomes more conscious and appreciative of her fullest feminine nature. Once she arrives at this position and builds the necessary bridges uniting all four realms, it becomes progressively easier for her to cross back and forth on any of these bridges at will.

Because the hero myth is the dominant myth of our society, it is held up as the model for both sexes. It is natural and normal for men to take the clockwise journey; by doing so, a man can move toward wholeness. Unfortunately, in a patriarchy, many women believe they, too, must take the masculine hero journey. Instead of following their natural path deeper into the feminine, they avoid self-examination. They remain in the exterior world, often rejecting the marvelous feminine world of the Mother — which is their birthright and is meant to be their reward — and jumping directly into the Father's world. But because this masculine journey is not the truest expression of the feminine nature, it does not yield the expected rewards.

This, as June Singer, the Jungian analyst, has so aptly phrased it, is the sadness of the successful woman. As hard as she may work and as successful as she may be, she cannot start her journey to wholeness by becoming individuated in the outer world as the masculine hero does, because her natural path leads in the other direction. And so, despairing of ever becoming individuated, and feeling guilty because she has neglected her relationships (something that masculine heroes seem to find far easier to do in their early years), a woman may give up on her work and decide to focus only on relationships in the outer world. But this does not satisfy her either, because she remains ashamed of herself for not living up to her full potential. If only she had known that the answer was to journey within to the island!

I tried to live the hero myth for many years. I was a teacher, first in elementary schools, then at the university level. I also produced children's television shows for two years. People told me I was good at these things, and I believed them. I got approval from my students and peers and friends, which made me feel pretty good about myself.

But what no one knew, what I rarely dared admit even to myself, was that there was not much about this kind of work that I really enjoyed. It was always difficult for me to get up in the mornings, always an effort to step into the shower and get myself dressed. Much of the time I actually dreaded the day ahead, and I gave myself pep talks on the way to work, reminding myself that I was prepared, that I would do just fine, and that it would be over soon. I assumed everyone felt this way about their work and that the secret was to ignore your real feelings and just get tough and get on with it. After teaching a three-hour class, I usually had a headache. By the time the day was over, I felt drained of all energy. I lived that way for many years, hiding the truth from myself and others.

By the time I earned my doctorate, I had been doing island

work for about two years. I had gotten in touch with many of my inner feminine and masculine aspects and was learning to value my individuality, but I was not yet ready to give up on the hero myth; it was all I knew, all I trusted. I wanted a full-time, tenure-earning teaching position, but there was nothing available in my field at any of the local universities.

I was in the middle of another difficult conflict. I could stay in Orlando, where I would never be more than an adjunct professor, or I could look for a job in another town or another state. But if I accepted a job elsewhere, I would either have to move there by myself or convince my husband and children, who were happy right where we were, to move with me.

After a few discussions with my husband, I realized he would never be happy if he left Orlando. He loved his work and life-style. What was I to do? I knew by then that my happiness was as important as his, and it seemed to me then that the only way I could be happy was as a full-time professor. But my needs to nurture my family relationships and to promote the happiness and best interests of my husband and children were equally powerful. This was another fork in the road, another classic dilemma between my masculine need for individuation and my feminine need for relationship.

Finally, after much prayer, poetry-writing, and contemplation, I decided that my need to maintain a close, intimate connection with my husband and children was more important to me than my need to be a professor. I would seek work within a fifty-mile radius of my home in Orlando. I would simply have to trust that something would change — either the job market or my ambitions. And if nothing did, if I never got the kind of teaching job I wanted, so be it!

This was the first time I found the courage to challenge the hero myth, the first time I was willing to fail at the heroic task I had assigned myself: to climb to the top of my profession. The idea that perhaps I didn't have to be a hero was very new to me. What a surprise it was to discover that, once I made a conscious choice to be true to my real needs instead of adhering to the hero myth, my dominant feeling was not pain or self-pity. It was relief!

For me, this decision was a bridge between individuation and relationship — a middle way that honored both without going to extremes in either direction. And so I continued to teach as an adjunct, and I continued working on my relationships. Most important, I continued my inner work.

As I got more in touch with my unconscious, I discovered an aspect of my personality that I had been ignoring for years. I had thought there was something wrong with this "other" part of me for not enjoying my job; secretly I was afraid she was lazy and didn't really want to work at all. Or maybe she was so terribly flawed that she would never be able to enjoy anything — maybe she was just destined to be unhappy. But I decided to face the truth, no matter how bad it might be, and I found that this "other" was not so bad after all. In fact, she was my very best friend, for she wanted to get me out of work that was wrong for me and into the kind of work I was made for.

As long as I worked out of a blind, unconscious need to bolster my old, childish ego by proving that I could succeed at the hero myth, I was dissatisfied, tired, and uncreative. But once I quit pretending to be happy with this journey and allowed my real personality to unfold, once I began to pursue my true interests without apology or guilt, I rediscovered writing, especially writing about human psychological and spiritual development. By honoring my "masculine" need for individuation but allowing it to happen in a "feminine" way (through inner work), and by honoring my "feminine" need to nurture my relationships, I built a bridge that unified these two opposing aspects of my true Self and brought me to the right kind of work for me in the outer "masculine" world.

The difference between the way I used to approach my work and the way I view it now is amazing to me. As I've worked on this book, I've looked forward to each day with eager anticipation; I seem to have boundless energy. Some days I write straight for eight, nine, or ten hours, and even then I have to drag myself away from my computer! At other times I feel the need to back off from writing for a while and read or relax. I no longer worry about losing my motivation during these times; I trust that my unconscious knows what is best for me and will let me know when I'm ready to write again.

In fact, I rarely worry about my work at all any more because I know my conscious ego does not have to have all the answers or solve all the problems. I don't *have* to be creative; my unconscious has all the creativity I'll ever need. I just have to stay in touch with her and wait for her to help me by means of such things as dreams, intuitions, instincts, fantasies, or ideas that seem to pop into my head out of nowhere.

What a relief to know I don't have to do it all! What bliss to simply relax and let it happen. I never knew it was possible to find such joy in work. I never dreamed there could be such pleasure in everyday living.

As I write about the feminine journey, something occurs to me. Could this be the reason why so many women live longer than men? Because the feminine still has important contributions to make to the outer world long after masculine outer work has been accomplished?

Mother Teresa, Golda Meir, Florence Nightingale, Indira Gandhi, Anne Morrow Lindbergh — these women fully experienced their pain and acquired self-knowledge before beginning their life-changing work in the outer world. Their island ordeals fortified them with such courage, strength, and integrity that when they returned to the world they were able to endure the challenges awaiting them with the kind of grace and confidence that only comes from having *gnosis,* the inner experience of knowing the utter truth and rightness about their life and their destiny. A masculine hero may make his contribution to the world on sheer ego strength, determination, daring deeds, and youthful energy before going within to discover his Self and complete his journey to wholeness; but I believe that a woman who is called to wholeness must acquire *gnosis* before she is truly ready for the world. Maybe this is the reason why many women make important contributions to the outer world in their later years, after they have endured, suffered, and survived the most important work of all: the transforming work of the island and the building of the bridge.

Not all examples of feminine transformation are nearly so dramatic as these, but every woman who undergoes an inner transformation on the island obtains there what she needs to fulfill her destiny. Her destiny may not be to acquire riches or worldly acclaim or to influence history. But, regardless of what she does with her life, when she builds the bridge that connects her inner Self to the outside world, she will find work there that is right for her and that brings deep inner peace and satisfaction.

What more is there to hope for in this life?

22

Trust Thyself

APOLLO'S MOTTO WAS "KNOW THYSELF." To this ancient motto I would like to add one other admonition that seems to complete it: "Trust Thyself." When combined, these two phrases create a credo to guide the inner, feminine phase of the journey to authenticity and wholeness: "Have the courage to look deep and the boldness to act upon what you see."

Each of us has an inner vision, perfectly suited to our personalities and deepest instincts, of how to be true to ourselves. Some women so deeply trust their inner vision that they are capable of acting on it with an unusual amount of self-sufficiency and independence. Women like this rarely feel the need to rely heavily on others for advice, guidance, or affirmation. Often their vision is more unconventional than most, so sometimes they have the farthest and most difficult road to travel away from traditional norms in order to reach their goals. But because of their strong faith in themselves, which is, in fact, faith in a Divine Being who has ordained the inner plan for their lives, they trust themselves instinctively to do the right thing at the right time.

Women like this remind me of cats. Until eighteen years ago, I had no experience with cats. Then one day my husband brought home a kitten for our three-year-old daughter, who had just had her tonsils out.

"What will you name her?" her father asked as he presented our daughter with a tortoise shell-tinted ball of fluff.

Julie didn't hesitate a second. "Miss Lottie," she said, with the utter confidence of innocent youth.

Miss Lottie? Where in the world did that come from? we wondered. But there was no doubt that Miss Lottie was the name of the tiny feminine creature who entered our lives that day and who has taught me many lessons over the last eighteen years.

For example, when Miss Lottie was younger, she spent hours outdoors stalking birds, squirrels, or lizards. With infinite patience, she waited for her prey, with no certainty that she would ever catch it and no apparent remorse if she didn't.

Miss Lottie also demonstrates what it means to have instinctive trust in herself through her perseverance despite difficult obstacles. No matter how many times I pick her up off the kitchen table and set her on the floor, she always hops right back up! She believes in the importance of her goal and simply will not be deterred. If thwarted, she takes an alternative route, even to the point of risking my disapproval and misunderstanding, because of her confidence in herself and her indifference to ideas about what she "should" be doing. Although her independence can be annoying to others, it is an admirable quality, both in cats and in women.

Miss Lottie can also be strongly competitive when necessary because she takes pride in her rights and her abilities. Even now, when she is so old and frail that the slightest nudge can tip her over, she still manages to force our little dog, Peri, to leave my lap so she can place her own softly purring body in this choice spot. She knows what she is entitled to, and she isn't afraid to do what she must to get it.

One of Miss Lottie's most wonderful qualities is her sensuousness. Sometimes she wants to be touched, stroked, and cuddled. Then she shows her pure pleasure by purring contentedly. At other times, she luxuriates in just the right sunny spot on the floor, or in a long, leisurely stretch after a restful nap, or in a loving, gentle grooming of her fur. What a marvelous, pleasurable thing a body is, her every gesture seems to say.

A woman can learn a great deal about being a more complete person from a cat, or from women who are as strong and sensuous and self-sufficient as Miss Lottie. She can learn how to trust herself. By affirming her patience, self-sufficiency, independence, perseverance, competitiveness, confidence, sensuality, and creativity, a woman can begin to remove the stumbling blocks to spiritual and psychological growth that stereotypes from the patriarchal world have thrown in her path. This transformation is made possible by her growing respect for a feminine vision, by her expanding perspective on acceptable feminine behaviors, and by the self-affirmation that comes from recognizing the feminine aspect of the Divine Being in her purest and truest inner voice.

When she learns to listen to her own voice and confidently follow her own instincts, a woman builds a bridge from her old, conforming self to her real feminine Self. When I began to listen to myself, I discovered that my real femininity is, like Miss Lottie, far more sensuous and mysterious and delightful than any "feminine" stereotype could be. Here are a few of the things I have learned to trust about myself:

I find that I love the night. The darker it gets outside, the more contented and settled, alive and real I become inside. I love not being able to see what is ahead, the sense that anything can happen, the unpredictability, the complexity, the spontaneity, the danger, the vastness, the messiness, the divine mystery of night.

In daylight I tend to think with masculine logic and reason, but in moonlight my thinking becomes more intuitive, subtle, and infinitely more creative. My best ideas always come at night. That is why I keep a pad of paper and a pen beside my bed. Most of the ideas for this book came to me just before I fell asleep. And many of the metaphors, stories, and anecdotes came to me during my dreams or after I had been awakened in the middle of the night by a dream.

I love to be near water and have unconsciously sought to live near bodies of water all my life. When I'm near enough to the ocean to hear the pounding of the waves, I become acutely aware of my body and its physical senses, and I feel deeply grateful to be alive. I'm at my most sensual near water, and if I'm near the water at night, I can become positively vibrant!

Sometimes I feel mysteriously connected to animals, plants, places, and even inanimate objects. Then I carefully monitor every thought, every movement, every utterance, for I know that all these things make a difference. At times like this it seems to me as if everything in the world embodies a quality of life like my own. The only difference is that I can't discern it with my senses. But somehow I can feel it.

I need to hear music and I love to dance. Dancing brings my body and mind into delightful harmony, and I'm rarely happier or more at peace than when I'm moving my body in just the right way to just the right kind of music.

Despite the prevailing biases about how women should look, I like my gray hair. I think it looks good on me. For me, it represents a blend between dark and light, which is the way I used to view the world. Now I prefer to seek the middle way, a hard-won path of silver that only comes with maturity and wisdom.

I am no longer comfortable with a work ethic that requires me to prove my worth by "doing" and rushing about. This hurried way of life makes me anxious. Now, as a self-employed writer, I work when I want to, rest when I feel tired, and spend quiet time communicating with my unconscious Self.

One way I do this is by stopping throughout the day and contemplating my inner condition whenever I notice strong feelings or physical sensations. A second way is by writing, and a third way is by paying attention to my dreams. Especially through the messages of my dreams, my Self has gently guided me toward meaningful work, peace, self-confidence, and a sense of purpose about my life. She has granted me the companionship of inner guides and authorities who know and love me for who I truly am and who will never desert me, no matter what lies ahead.

I have hope and even a sense of anticipation about the years ahead, for I know that, having made a transition from a single-minded focus on work and relationships in the outer world to a focus on my interior world, I have more trust that my inner life will provide me with satisfaction as I grow older.

I've learned that my mind and my body seem to be attuned to a rhythm that coincides with the waxing and waning of the moon and the ebb and flow of the tides. It is a rhythm that repeats itself again and again in a cyclical pattern. It begins (if any one phase can be seen as a beginning) with a time of lethargy and inner discomfort when I need to be quiet and withdraw and rest. This time is like the darkest phase of the moon, when it hides its face from the earth and all her inhabitants. Gradually, like the moon, I enter a time of transition when I seem to gain increasing energy and momentum day by day. I grow fuller and fuller until suddenly one day I feel as if I'm on top of the world and can't imagine ever being sad or low or lacking again. Yet slowly I fade and lose more and more of my glow until once again I feel nibbles of anxiety and discomfort and can no longer remember what fullness feels like.

This cycle repeats itself every month and, on a broader scale, every several months, roughly coinciding with the seasons. I've even discovered a cycle in my life that seems to run its full course every ten years. After years of becoming more aware of my personal rhythms, I've finally learned neither to dread the passing of the high time, for it always comes again, nor to expect the low time to last forever, for it, too, always passes.

I've learned that the more I trust my body, the more efficient it has become at sending me messages about the state of my being. I find that a headache or stomachache comes soon after the event that caused it, and it usually disappears just as quickly, as soon as I deal with the source of my discomfort.

Learning to trust my body has been an incredible blessing to me because it shows me when my personality is out of balance. From the lessons learned during my island work, I know that my body doesn't want me to be a perfectionist and that I need to spend a great deal of time alone. I make less effort to please people I don't really like, and I involve myself in few activities I don't enjoy. I can let go of my pride and allow other people to help me with things that are difficult for me.

And I can see the difference between the things I was doing just to please or impress others and the things that are truly right for me: My body never rebels when I'm doing something I love. By paying attention to my body, I'm learning to relax and enjoy the things I need to do, to rest when I feel tired, and to say no to things that are wrong for me.

The treasures of feminine wisdom, wisdom that has been hidden for centuries, are resurrected from the unconscious and brought back into the conscious world by means of the bridges that each of us, both women and men, constructs within our personalities. Learning to appreciate the dark, enigmatic side of life; becoming aware of the unimaginable riches to be found in the vast, watery, unconscious depths of the human mind; knowing ourselves to be inseparable from all of creation; being able to lose ourselves in the delightful harmony between the body and the soul; valuing our inner qualities over outer appearances; taking the time to stay in touch with the unconscious; honoring the rhythms of our life; loving and learning from our bodies — these are only a few of the many contributions that feminine wisdom can make to help us unravel the mystery of human existence. There are so many more . . . if we will only learn to trust ourselves.

23

What Does a "Whole" Person Look Like?

YEARS AGO WHEN I TAUGHT THIRD GRADE in a small country school, there was an unusual little boy in my class. He came from a large, poor family who made their living selling the fish they caught on a nearby lake. He was small for his age, but I never knew him to shy away from a confrontation with the bigger boys if they started something. His clothes had been well-worn by several older brothers, his brown hair stuck out in stiff, uneven spikes, and sometimes he didn't smell very good. But if he considered himself deprived in any way, he never showed it, for he was the happiest, most well-adjusted child I've ever known.

One day a friend of mine visited my class. She watched as, during snack time, this boy popped up from his seat, walked over to my desk, opened his grubby little fist, and dropped four slightly soggy corn chips onto my desk. On the way back to his seat he gave a frisky little hop in the air before he sat back down to his snack, grinning to himself as he enjoyed the inner rewards of his generous, spontaneous gift to me.

"My, he's full of himself," my friend commented with a smile. She never forgot that scene and enjoyed telling people how I, whom she considered to be somewhat fastidious, had summoned all my courage and eaten the chips that had dropped from his grimy fingers. But in truth, it had not occurred to me that they might be dirty, and I ate them without giving a thought to hygiene, for I was pondering the wonder of the amazing fullness of being of this delightful elfin creature.

Full of himself. That is exactly what he was: proud, lively, confident, tough, creative, feisty, independent, open, optimistic, trusting, accepting of me and all his classmates, spontaneous, playful, affectionate. He was pleased to be exactly who he was, happily expectant to see what would happen next, and as blissfully innocent as a puppy.

We all begin our lives with that kind of innocence, but few of us retain it for long. Most of my eight-year-old students had begun to lose it by the time they came to me. Occasionally I would get one who had already become hostile and cynical, or another who was painfully timid and fearful. This is part of what it means to be human: We get to experience bliss in the safety of our childhood castles just long enough to know it exists, then we are robbed of our innocence and forced to spend the rest of our lives searching for what we have lost.

We lose our bliss partly because of things that happen to us at home and at school, and partly because of some early choices we make that shape our personalities in certain directions, toward certain preferences, until we get stuck on one side of the bridge in behavior patterns that lead us away from our original totality. Being stuck in one-sidedness robs us of our full potential and prevents us from experiencing the blissful completeness of youth, a time when we were innocently connected to our instincts and emotions, when we felt free to act with joyous, honest spontaneity instead of rigid habit.

We do not have to be one-sided. It is possible for us to live full, well-rounded, blissful lives and build the bridge that leads to fullness. For those who find it, the place of deliverance looks amazingly like the castle we left long ago. Moreover, we return to a state that strongly resembles our original innocence. But this time there is an important difference — the difference between the puppy and the person, the princess and the queen. For we have left the security of thick castle walls and wandered through the wilderness following an elusive bear. We have faced death on the island where we have made peace with our dragons, and we have built a bridge from unconsciousness to consciousness. In our earlier state, our innocence was characterized by a blissful ignorance; our newly acquired knowledge and awareness typify a fuller, more meaningful innocence.

Becoming aware of our unconscious Self is the task for both men and women on this earth. Each step we take closes the gaps between our conscious selves and the unknown aspects of our personalities, and brings us ever closer to a unique new personality that continually expands into wholeness as long as we proceed with our inner work. When we begin to experience the positive results of these inner bridges, we feel as fresh and hopeful as a newborn baby. It feels like we are emerging into an improved version of the kind of innocence my little third-grade student had. Once again we are creative, open, confident, independent, spontaneous, enthusiastic about life, and excited about the possibilities of each new day. Once again we are delightfully full of ourselves.

But wholeness is not just about being full of ourselves because we are becoming individuated. It is also about relationship — about building meaningful connections to our true inner Self, to others, to all of creation, to the Divine Being. In order to approach wholeness, isolation is necessary for a time, but we cannot remain forever on an island. We need relationships with others to show us who we are so that we can become differentiated from them. And we need relationships to teach us the meaning of love.

Although the concept of wholeness is basic to psychological and spiritual thought, it is really only an ideal because, unlike the dramatic, once-in-a-lifetime emergence of the chicken from the egg, wholeness is a gradual, never-ending process, not an identifiable product. It is a process of learning how to cross back and forth on a bridge, both flowing into the outer world and ebbing into the inner world; here responding to the needs of others, there tending to our own. Back and forth, around and around we go, like the circulation of blood through the vessels of our bodies or like the movement of air we inhale into our lungs and then exhale into the universe in a never-ending cycle of life.

The scarcity of models makes it hard to describe a whole person, but it helps to have an idea of what one might look like. Whole people:

- love themselves
- can laugh at themselves
- risk being true to themselves
- are involved in meaningful work
- balance outer work with inner work
- look for the good and hope for the best
- are creative and original (not necessarily artistic)
- are comfortable with their masculine and feminine aspects
- develop a personal ethic based on love for self and others
- enjoy food, rest, work, play, learning, mentoring, and sex (those authentically called to celibacy not included)
- sometimes experience ecstasy at the beauty of creation
- experience anger, anxiety, fear, sadness, and guilt
- have a deeply meaningful spiritual life
- accept responsibility for their choices
- know they don't have all the answers

- respond spontaneously to life
- love their bodies
- love the truth
- love life
- love
- affirm others
- don't use others
- don't need to impress others
- suffer when others are suffering
- are cautious about dispensing advice
- don't blame others for their unhappiness
- respect children, animals, nature, and mystery
- have honest, intimate relationships with others
- judge others by their behavior, not their gender
- recognize the hurt and fear that underlie the unattractive words and behaviors of obnoxious people
- have forgiven their parents for their mistakes
- put their trust in the unknowable "Other"
- don't allow others to manipulate them
- don't make promises they can't keep
- can say no without feeling guilty
- are willing to confront others
- listen more than they talk
- see others as teachers
- love others

The goal of the feminine quest is not perfection; it is completion. It is this interpretation of wholeness, as a continuing process of facing and integrating and making peace with every aspect of our true Selves — the good and the bad, and the masculine and the feminine — that must be addressed in today's new myths. If healing is to occur, we must be exposed to feminine stories about the way to salvation, and we must learn to value them as much as we have loved the hero myth.

I'll sing you a song about the feminine quest for wholeness.

How does a woman find her Self?

She honors the truth about her personality with its strengths and weaknesses, its saints and demons, its natural aptitudes and forgivable flaws.

She honors her feminine body that was created for the purpose of protecting, nurturing, and giving birth to new life. This is a real body of flesh and blood, an awesome body that is the incarnation of life, a beautiful body of rounded softness, a terrible body that is subject to the decay of death.

She honors her soul, that part of herself that is most in touch with the unconscious realm of instincts, intuitions, fantasies, emotional rhythms, and dreams. This is where she discovers her unique creativity.

She honors her spirituality in both its feminine and masculine aspects. She honors masculine spirituality, which finds expression in conscious attempts to approach the divine through words, prayer, doctrines, scriptural studies, and meaningful rituals within the bounds of organized religion. And she honors her more instinctive, feminine spirituality, which often manifests in personally meaningful rituals and feelings of awe and connectedness that are experienced through music and bodily movement and in physical, natural settings. The feminine approaches the Divine Being when she dances alone in a moonlit forest cathedral beneath over-arching branches, when she listens to the music of the uni-

verse in an island sanctuary, or when she swims at midnight in a watery temple beneath the waves.

She honors her heart, her tender compassion for all humanity, her sense of deep connection to others, her emotions, her feelings, her need to preserve and nurture life, her power to sacrifice everything for those she loves — and her ability to wound them.

She honors her mind. She establishes a relationship with her masculine way of thinking and acquires the courage, knowledge, and energy to actively pursue her goals and ideals so that she may persevere in her quest for individuation. And she respects her special feminine kind of wisdom — the wisdom of the understanding heart.

Finally, she is willing to suffer. She endures the suffering that always accompanies the pursuits of individuality and of intimacy with others. And she deals with the rage that comes from seeking to discover and honor her true identity in a world that does not value the feminine.

When we can accept our full Selves, we are ready for our destiny. When we conduct the necessary inner work to overcome our resistances, we unify the opposites in our personalities and are true to our Selves. We make the myriad connections between our conscious and unconscious worlds, our inner and outer lives, our liked and feared qualities, and the feminine and masculine aspects of our authentic, whole Selves. When we move freely among conscious choice, creativity, relationship, and individuality, we are building the bridge, creating the way to wholeness.

Selected Bibliography

MY FAVORITE TEACHERS HAVE ALWAYS BEEN BOOKS. They have a marvelous sense of timing. They are quiet, gentle, patient, loving, and wise, and they never judge the student. In my life, the right book has always had a way of popping up just when I needed it.

The following is a list of some of the books that were most meaningful to me in writing *The Bridge to Wholeness*. I have grouped them into three general categories, but some refuse my system of classification and could easily fit into all three. Favorite books are like favorite people — so complex and unique they defy simple description.

Understanding Dreams

Cirlot, J.E. *A Dictionary of Symbols.* 2d Ed. New York: Philosophical Library, 1971.

> The study of symbols is an important tool in decoding the mysterious language of the unconscious. This is a thorough listing of the underlying meanings of symbols that appear in dreams, visions, art, mythology, religion, archaeology, and literature. I have turned to it many times when I have dreamed about something for which I could find no immediate associations in my own experience or conscious thoughts. Like a cafeteria, this book offers a broad range of possibilities from which the dreamer may find the exact morsel to satisfy a particular appetite at just the moment when she needs it.

Clift, Jean Dalby, and Wallace B. Clift. *Symbols of Transformation in Dreams.* New York: Crossroad Publishing, 1987.

> This great little book is one of the first I read about dream interpretation and one of my favorites. It gives a clear, concise explanation of Carl Jung's dream theory and how it applies to individuals.

Garfield, Patricia, Ph.D. *Women's Bodies, Women's Dreams.* New York: Ballantine Books, 1988.

> A good book written by a clinical psychologist and dream expert about how and why women's dreams differ from those of men. Garfield discusses the phases of a woman's life and shows how women can get in touch with the meaning of their lives through their dreams.

Jung, C.G. *Dreams*. Princeton, NJ: Princeton University Press, 1974.

> Jung had a deep reverence for the unconscious and for the ability of dreams to communicate the workings of the unconscious to the conscious mind. Here he explains the nature of dreams, how they can be analyzed, and the significance of certain dream symbols including numbers, mandalas, and symbols of the Self. This compilation of some of Jung's writings on dreams may be hard going for those who are unfamiliar with Jungian psychology and terminology.

Matthews, Boris, trans. *The Herder Symbol Dictionary*. Wilmette, IL: Chiron Publications, 1986.

> Another excellent resource for understanding the meaning of symbols. Though less extensive than Cirlot's dictionary, it is often more concise, and it contains many entries and interpretations not included in Cirlot. I like having at least two such resources. Both have been very helpful to me.

McDonald, Phoebe. *Dreams: Night Language of the Soul*. New York: Continuum, 1988.

> A clear, thorough introduction to the interpretation of dreams, written mostly from a Jungian perspective. McDonald's explanations of the mechanisms of the unconscious and the aspects of the inner Self are helpful to the novice in dream interpretation.

Sanford, John A. *Dreams: God's Forgotten Language.* San Francisco: Harper & Row, 1989.

> I have a special affinity for Sanford's work because he seems to struggle with the same kinds of questions I do. As an Episcopalian priest and a Jungian analyst, his specialty is exploring the common threads between Christianity and Jungian psychology, and he writes clearly and succinctly about the connections between these two fields. In this book he lays a biblical foundation for the importance of dream work as a way of bringing us closer to our Selves and to the kingdom of God.

Segaller, Stephen, and Merrill Berger. *The Wisdom of the Dream: The World of C.G. Jung.* Boston: Shambhala, 1989.

> For those who are interested in knowing more about Carl Jung, this book, based on a British television series, describes his life and psychological theories through the eyes of some of his students, patients, and followers. This book is more of a testimony to the genius of the man who recognized the importance and nature of dreams than a text about dreams. It depicts the unusual world view and vision of a remarkable man and describes how his search for meaning has enriched the lives of seekers everywhere.

Signell, Karen A., Ph.D. *Wisdom of the Heart: Working with Women's Dreams.* New York: Bantam Books, 1990.

> A wise, wonderful book about the dreams of women, and a personal favorite. Written from a Jungian perspective, this book demonstrates how women can work with their dreams to get in touch with their inner wisdom.

Mythology, Fairy Tales, and Human Psychology

Bettelheim, Bruno. *The Uses of Enchantment: The Meaning and Importance of Fairy Tales.* New York: Vintage Books, 1977.

> This classic volume is the first one I ever read that described the relationship between fairy tales and human psychology. It has been a major influence in my teaching and thinking, and has provided me with a valuable tool for understanding and describing the meaning of my life. As a child psychologist, Bettelheim focuses specifically on the enormous value of fairy tales as a means of helping children deal with their inner conflicts. His method is to relate several popular fairy tales, describe the underlying issues and instructive values in each, and show how hearing these stories can help children recognize important truths and cope with normal developmental problems. Bettelheim's model of extracting psychological truths from fairy tales provided a primary inspiration for the format I followed in my own book.

Murray, Alexander S. *Who's Who in Mythology: A Classic Guide to the Ancient World.* 2nd Ed. New York: Bonanza Books, 1988.

> Unlike most of his predecessors, who tended to focus almost exclusively on the masculine deities in the Greek and Roman pantheons, Murray devotes equal space to many of the goddesses. Three chapters in this new edition deal with Norse, German, Hindu, and Egyptian mythology. Although it does not delve into the ancient mythologies in which goddess reverence was at its height, this book is a good resource for the more familiar mythological characters, symbols, and motifs.

Nelson, Gertrud Mueller. *Here All Dwell Free: Stories to Heal the Wounded Feminine.* New York: Doubleday, 1991.

> Besides Bettelheim, Nelson was the other major inspiration for the format of my book. At a conference, I heard her tell the stories of "The Handless Maiden" and "Briar Rose" and powerfully describe their relevance for the lives of modern women. Although I had already read Bettelheim's book and had taught children's literature for many years, when I used Nelson's technique in a speech to a group of adults, I realized the potency of fairy tales as communicators of truth about individual lives. In her wonderful book, Nelson tells these same two stories. I am deeply touched by her beautiful use of language, her haunting telling of classic stories, and her remarkable insight into feminine experience. This book is a must for all women who seek self-knowledge.

Singer, June. *Androgyny: The Opposites Within.* Boston: Sigo Press, 1989.

> I read Singer's book after I had finished writing mine. First published in 1976, it has had a strong influence on many of the other writers I have read. If you would like to trace the roots of androgyny back to its earliest, ancient expression of human wholeness and forward into the present and perhaps even the future, this is the book to read. It is magnificent.

Stone, Merlin. *Ancient Mirrors of Womanhood: A Treasury of Goddess and Heroine Lore from Around the World.* Boston: Beacon Press, 1984.

> This is a marvelous resource, the most complete I have ever seen on feminine mythology. Stone treats all her female subjects with the reverence and respect they were accorded in the ancient world that existed before the patriarchal Greek and Roman eras, which is where most other collections begin.

Von Franz, Marie-Louise. *Interpretation of Fairy Tales*. Dallas: Spring Publications, 1970.

> Von Franz believes that all fairy tales are attempts to describe the Self. For that reason they are, like dreams, important psychological resources. In this valuable book she describes a method of psychological interpretation and demonstrates how to use it. She discusses the shadow, anima, and animus in fairy tales. The methods she presents can also be applied to dream analysis.

Walker, Barbara G. *The Woman's Encyclopedia of Myths and Secrets*. New York: Harper & Row, 1983.

> A fascinating resource that fills in many gaps and corrects many of the biases of the patriarchal perspective of history. An astonishing collection of superlative, thorough research about women's history and the feminine principle, this work offers a refreshing and desperately needed balance to our long tradition of masculine one-sidedness.

The Inner Journey to the Feminine and Sacred Psychology

Birkhauser-Oeri, Sibylle. *The Mother: Archetypal Image in Fairy Tales*. Toronto: Inner City Books, 1988.

> A marvelous study of the power and the positive and negative aspects of the feminine principle as it is made manifest in fairy tales. Rich in symbols and imagery, this book discusses psychic issues that influence both women and men and the impact these inner issues have on the outer world.

Bolen, Jean Shinoda, M.D. *Goddesses in Everywoman: A New Psychology of Women.* New York: Harper Colophon Books, 1984.
> Brilliant and revolutionary, this book was too good to put down and an absolute revelation to me. I have never read anything that has so powerfully affirmed me as an individual or made me so proud and grateful to be a woman.

de Castillejo, Irene. *Knowing Woman.* New York: G.P. Putnam's Sons, 1973.
> I loved this book about the differences between the masculine and the feminine and the relationships between the two in the inner and outer worlds.

Duerk, Judith. *Circle of Stones: Woman's Journey to Herself.* San Diego: LuraMedia, 1989.
> When I had finished writing my book and begun to look for a publisher, Jungian analyst Karen Signell suggested that I submit it to the publisher of *Circle of Stones.* I was overwhelmed by this extraordinary book that pays such badly needed homage to feminine truth in so few words — all of them quotable. Duerk and I have come to the same understandings and are saying the same things about the feminine quest. This humble little book contains a wealth of wisdom that is as nourishing to the feminine spirit as a lavish banquet. In it, I have found affirmation for my own journey, and in its author I have found a soul mate.

Hannah, Barbara. *Striving towards Wholeness.* Boston: Sigo Press, 1988.
> Hannah, a Jungian analyst, studied the works of Robert Louis Stevenson, Mary Webb, and the Brontës to understand how the psychological characteristics of their creative work reflected their psychological development. I found this book to be full of helpful insights into my own journey.

Harding, M. Esther. *The Way of All Women*. Boston & London: Shambhala, 1990 reprint.

First written in 1933, this is a wonderful study of feminine psychology, based on the work of Jung. Some of the issues Harding discusses are work, relationships, marriage, and motherhood. Even though times have changed, it seems that the human spirit changes much more slowly, and most of Harding's insights have remarkable relevance for women today.

Houston, Jean. *The Search for the Beloved: Journeys in Mythology and Sacred Psychology*. Los Angeles: Jeremy P. Tarcher, 1987.

After I read this book, I wrote on the title page: "Stupendous! Incredibly affirming. Very important!" The first part defines sacred psychology and offers guidelines for participating in ritual processes, preferably in a group setting. The remainder of the book describes these processes, which include body work and creative imagination, and suggests appropriate accompanying music, materials, and settings.

Johnson, Robert A. *Femininity Lost and Regained*. New York: Harper & Row, 1990.

A marvelous book by one of my favorite writers. Johnson is a wise and gentle Jungian analyst who gives compelling lectures and writes in much the same way as he speaks. He is particularly concerned about the loss of feminine qualities in women and men today. Using two myths as the basis for his discussion, he describes feminine values and illustrates the importance of reintegrating feminine energy into modern culture.

Johnson, Robert A. *Inner Work*. San Francisco: Harper & Row, 1986.

Johnson describes a four-step approach to dream work and a four-step approach to active imagination. Both are valuable, immensely rewarding ways of getting in touch with the unconscious.

Johnson, Robert A. *She: Understanding Feminine Psychology*. New York: Harper & Row, 1977.

An illuminating book that uses the myth of Psyche and Amor to describe the feminine journey to individuation and to illustrate the special gifts that the feminine brings to life.

Jones, Alan. *Soul Making: The Desert Way of Spirituality*. San Francisco: Harper & Row, 1985.

Jones, an Episcopalian priest, speaks to the spiritual journeyer who wishes to live with passion and is willing to make new beginnings in a never-ending journey to the kingdom of God. Soul making involves a willingness to depart from group identification and journey to the desert (an island will do just as well) where we separate ourselves from the familiar. There the ego dies so that we can grow into a larger awareness of God, which is comprised of the trinity of absolute identity, absolute unity, and absolute freedom. Another version of an archetypal theme described from a unique perspective, this book provides an excellent explication of the underlying connections among theology, spirituality, and psychology.

Jung, C.G. *Modern Man in Search of a Soul*. San Diego: Harcourt Brace, Jovanovich, 1933.

A brilliant work by a brilliant pioneer into the largely unexplored realm of the soul.

Keyes, Margaret Frings. *Inward Journey: Art as Therapy*. La Salle, IL, & London: Open Court, 1983.

> A great little handbook that describes several art exercises and strategies to help people work creatively through the crises of their lives. Keyes also suggests ways to amplify dreams through creative work. This is a wonderful resource for those who might enjoy using art as a means of achieving greater inner awareness — a method I highly recommend.

Murdock, Maureen. *The Heroine's Journey: Woman's Quest for Wholeness*. Boston & London: Shambhala, 1990.

> Although the theme of this book is very similar to that of my book, these two expressions of the feminine journey create different pictures in much the same way that two artists interpret the same landscape in unique ways. For example, Murdock gives special attention to women's rejection of the feminine, including the rejection of the personal mother, and the problems involved in healing the mother-daughter split. This topic will be of special interest to women who have suffered from difficult relationships with their mothers.

Neumann, Erich. *The Great Mother: An Analysis of the Archetype*. Bollingen Series, no. 47. Princeton, NJ: Princeton University Press, 1955.

> A book of immense breadth of treatment and depth of scholarly research. It contains two hundred fifty-nine illustrations of aspects of the Great Mother, created by those who have had reverence for the feminine aspect of the deity from ancient times into the contemporary era. While it does not deal with the psychic phases of feminine transformation in individuals, it does thoroughly describe the multifaceted nature of a fundamental archetype that underlies the psychological history of women and men living today.

Nicholson, Shirley, ed. *The Goddess Re-Awakening: The Feminine Principle Today.* Wheaton, IL: Theosophical Publishing House, 1989.

> A wonderful compilation of important essays describing the reemergence of reverence for the feminine principle in contemporary consciousness. My favorites are Stephan Hoeller's discussion of "Sophia: The Gnostic Archetype of Feminine Soul-Wisdom," June Singer's incredible essay on "The Sadness of the Successful Woman," and Rabbi Leah Novick's compelling description of Schechinah, the Jewish goddess.

Pearson, Carol S., Ph.D. *The Hero Within: Six Archetypes We Live By.* San Francisco: Harper & Row, 1989.

> Another excellent book about the inner journey with a unique slant. Pearson's categories of Innocent, Orphan, Wanderer, Warrior, Martyr, and Magician as necessary stages of growth to wholeness are astute and immensely helpful.

Peck, M. Scott, M.D. *The Road Less Traveled.* New York: Simon & Schuster, 1978.

> I read this book shortly after it was published, when I was becoming painfully conscious of my dissatisfaction with myself. It helped more than I can say to know that there was an explanation for my discomfort — to realize that I was not alone and that there was hope for those willing to undertake a difficult journey on a road for which there were few signposts and no maps. Thank you, Scott Peck, for showing me the forks in the road.

Phillips, Dorothy Berkley, Elizabeth Boyden Howes, and Lucille M. Nixon, eds. *The Choice Is Always Ours: The Classic Anthology on the Spiritual Way.* San Francisco: Harper Collins, 1989.

> A dear friend gave me this book and told me I would love it. She was right! It describes dimensions of spirituality that I had never before associated with reverence for the deity because I had never learned about them in church. It was affirming to discover that so many of my most profound spiritual tendencies have been experienced by other seekers throughout recorded history and sanctioned as valid experiences of the Divine Being. Thank you, Emmy, for your beautiful gift to me.

Sanford, John A. *The Invisible Partners: How the Male and Female in Each of Us Affects Our Relationships.* New York: Paulist Press, 1980.

> Like June Singer, Sanford recognizes the archetypal nature of androgyny. This illuminating book describes why it is so crucial to our relationships that each of us understand and accept the masculine and the feminine aspects of our personalities.

Sanford, John A. *The Kingdom Within: The Inner Meaning of Jesus' Sayings.* Rev. Ed. San Francisco: Harper & Row, 1987.

> One of my all-time favorite books. What a treasure Sanford is for Christians who cannot ignore inner voices that compel them to depart from simplistic interpretations of the Scriptures. Better than anyone else I know, Sanford describes why the spiritual and psychological journeys are really one and the same journey to wholeness.

Sewell, Marilyn, ed. *Cries of the Spirit: A Celebration of Women's Spirituality.* Boston: Beacon Press, 1991.

> A rich, beautiful collection of poetry and prose about the feminine experience of spirituality. A gift I will always treasure from special friends.

Woodman, Marion. *The Pregnant Virgin: A Process of Psychological Transformation.* Toronto: Inner City Books, 1985.

> A special book by a Jungian analyst about the feminine struggle to become conscious. Woodman's significant contribution in this book is her insight about the reasons for and solutions to the addictions of so many women to food, busyness, or drugs. Also important is her plea that women learn to respect the wisdom of our bodies.

© Jimm Roberts/Orlando

Jean Benedict Raffa, Ed.D.

Jean Benedict Raffa is the author of *Introduction to Television Literacy* as well as articles in such publications as the *Phi Delta Kappan, The Educational Forum, Parish Teacher,* and *The Home Altar.* A self-employed writer and public speaker, she has served on the faculties of the University of Central Florida, Stetson University, and Western Carolina University. Her teaching specialties include children's literature and language arts. She is also a former coordinator of children's programming for WFTV television station in Orlando, Florida.

She earned her doctorate in curriculum and instruction at the University of Florida. She has pursued her interests in psychology, religion, women's studies, and mythology through intensive individual study.

She lives with her husband in Maitland, Florida, where she collects antiques, tends a rose garden, and enjoys frequent visits from her daughter and son, both of whom attend Florida State University.

LuraMedia Publications

BANKSON, MARJORY ZOET
Braided Streams: *Esther and a Woman's Way of Growing*
Seasons of Friendship: *Naomi and Ruth as a Pattern*
"This Is My Body . . .": *Creativity, Clay, and Change*

BOHLER, CAROLYN STAHL
Prayer on Wings: *A Search for Authentic Prayer*

BOZARTH, ALLA RENEE
Womanpriest: *A Personal Odyssey (Rev. Ed.)*

GEIGER, LURA JANE
Astonish Me, Yahweh Leader's Guide

and **PATRICIA BACKMAN**
Braided Streams Leader's Guide

and **SUSAN TOBIAS**
Seasons of Friendship Leader's Guide

and **SANDY LANDSTEDT, MARY GECKELER, PEGGIE OURY**
Astonish Me, Yahweh!: *A Bible Workbook-Journal*

JEVNE, RONNA FAY
It All Begins With Hope: *Patients, Caretakers, and the Bereaved Speak Out*

and **ALEXANDER LEVITAN**
No Time for Nonsense: *Getting Well Against the Odds*

KEIFFER, ANN
Gift of the Dark Angel: *A Woman's Journey through Depression toward Wholeness*

LODER, TED
Eavesdropping on the Echoes: *Voices from the Old Testament*
Guerrillas of Grace: *Prayers for the Battle*
No One But Us: *Personal Reflections on Public Sanctuary*
Tracks in the Straw: *Tales Spun from the Manger*
Wrestling the Light: *Ache and Awe in the Human-Divine Struggle*

MEYER, RICHARD C.
One Anothering: *Biblical Building Blocks for Small Groups*

MILLETT, CRAIG
In God's Image: *Archetypes of Women in Scripture*

O'CONNOR, ELIZABETH
Search for Silence *(Revised Edition)*

RAFFA, JEAN BENEDICT
The Bridge to Wholeness: *A Feminine Alternative to the Hero Myth*

SAURO, JOAN
Whole Earth Meditation: *Ecology for the Spirit*

SCHAPER, DONNA
A Book of Common Power: *Narratives Against the Current*
Stripping Down: *The Art of Spiritual Restoration*

WEEMS, RENITA J.
Just a Sister Away: *A Womanist Vision of Women's Relationships in the Bible*

The Women's Series

BORTON, JOAN
Drawing from the Women's Well: *Reflections on the Life Passage of Menopause*

CARTLEDGE-HAYES, MARY
To Love Delilah: *Claiming the Women of the Bible*

DAHL, JUDY
River of Promise: *Two Women's Story of Love and Adoption*

DUERK, JUDITH
Circle of Stones: *Woman's Journey to Herself*

O'HALLORAN, SUSAN *and* **DELATTRE, SUSAN**
The Woman Who Lost Her Heart: *A Tale of Reawakening*

RUPP, JOYCE
The Star in My Heart: *Experiencing Sophia, Inner Wisdom*

SCHAPER, DONNA
Superwoman Turns 40: *The Story of One Woman's Intentions to Grow Up*

SCHNEIDER-AKER, KATHERINE
God's Forgotten Daughter: *A Modern Midrash . . . What If Jesus Had Been a Woman?*

LuraMedia, Inc. , 7060 Miramar Rd., Suite 104, San Diego, CA 92121
Books for Healing and Hope, Balance and Justice.